An INCIDENTAL CASUALTY

— The Experience of William Henry Randall in the American Civil War —

By

PETER E. SCHILLING

Copyright © 2012 by Peter E. Schilling
All Rights reserved.

DEDICATED TO

Matteline, Christopher, Caroline, Ava Ann, Eleanor Lynn, and William, descendants of William Henry Randall

TABLE OF CONTENTS

Remembering Ordinary Men	1
Grandpa	2
A Letter from Home	5
Civil War Begins	13
William Randall Joins the Army (Jan 23–Mar 27, 1864)	15
Along the Red River in Louisiana (March 28–April 7)	19
A Hard Fight at Pleasant Grove (April 8)	24
A Battle at Pleasant Hill (April 9)	27
Retreat after Victory (April 10–29)	31
Saving the Navy (April 30–May 22)	34
Pilgrims	41
Natchitoches	43
Summer in the Deep South (May 23–June 16)	47
A Journey to Vicksburg (June 17–July 22)	52
To Arkansas and Back (July 23–August 19)	59
Mobile Bay (August 20–September 8)	62
The War Continues (September 9–October 9)	67
Chasing Confederates (October 10–November 8)	72
Preparing for Winter (November 9–December 31)	76
A New Year and Another Journey (Jan 1–Feb 28, 1865)	83
A New Campaign (March 17–April 1, 1865)	85
William Randall Goes Home	89
The War Ends (after April 1, 1865)	91
Pilgrimage II	95
We Honor Their Memory	101
Appendices	107
Acknowledgements	108
Some Notes about Spelling	109
About the Army	111
Army Ranks	111
Organization of the Union Army	112
Glossary	113
Bibliography	118
People in This Writing	122
Members of William Henry Randall's Family	122
Officers and Soldiers	124
Others	128
Members of 161st NY Volunteer Infantry Regt	129
Index	138

REMEBERING ORDINARY MEN

Wars are fought by ordinary men. Most soldiers are privates who have no fame before joining the army, gain no distinction in battle, and are discharged to return to ordinary lives. Still, we honor them as war veterans.

In the American Civil War, most military units gained no lasting fame either. Newspapers reported their actions as the work of their commanders. Successes and failures of military units, of soldiers acting together, were ascribed to their generals: Pickett's charge at Gettysburg, and Sherman's march through Georgia. Most Army units were recruited from one geographic area — a city, a county, or a state senatorial or legislative district. The folks at home followed the military experience of family members and friends, "our hometown boys," with community pride and concern. As veterans, former soldiers remembered their units with pride. They spoke of the Iron Brigade, the Irish Brigade, the Fifth and Sixth Corps, and the Armies of Northern Virginia and of the Potomac. Some of their pride passed on to children and grandchildren. But most Civil War units are now forgotten.

Most Civil War battles and campaigns are also forgotten. Who remembers Donaldsonville, Brandy Station, Williamsburg, Sabine Pass, Kenesaw Mountain, Five Forks, or the Shenandoah Valley or Arkansas campaigns? Postwar gatherings of old veterans at Gettysburg grew into a tourist industry, which still thrives after the veterans are long gone. But the battle of Antietam Creek at nearby Sharpsburg, Maryland, produced more casualties than any other single day of the War. The Antietam battlefield and cemetery are quiet places with few tourists.

Nearly all of the Civil War soldiers, the military units in which they served, and the places where they fought and died, are forgotten except to scholars. The ordinary men who risked and sacrificed their lives are mostly unknown, even to their descendents. Yet their sacrifice still echoes in American politics as we debate the balance of responsibilities and rights between state and federal governments. It also echoes in how Americans see themselves: as Northerners or Southerners, Republicans or Democrats, blacks or whites. What ordinary men accomplished in our Civil War, was to sustain and clarify that continuing political experiment that we call "the United States of America." They did not see it so grandly.

From the Randall and McDaniel families, ten cousins, grandsons of Nehemiah Randall of Chenango Township, Broome County, New York, were among the three million ordinary men who served as soldiers for the Confederacy or the Union. Two cousins died. Three were wounded and permanently disabled. One returned home with a disabling illness. And of the four who had no physical injuries, even they suffered wounded memories from the terrors of war. Their family paid a terrible price to restore the United States of America.

This book is about one of those cousins, Private William Henry Randall, Company K, 161st New York Volunteer Infantry. He fought in battles at Pleasant Grove and Pleasant Hill in Louisiana, and at Spanish Fort in Alabama, in the Red River and Mobile Campaigns. He was wounded as the War ended, an incidental casualty in an unnecessary battle, away from the important actions that decided the outcome of the War. His wound partially disabled him from farming and justified a small pension. Other ailments from his war service caused him pain through the remaining thirty-three years of his life. He is buried under a stone that tells us his company and regiment.

During the year 1864, Private Randall kept a small diary. The entries do not reveal an articulate man. Instead, they show us his ordinariness. But the fact that he kept the diary tells us that he understood the importance of his service in the War. For William Randall, and for his cousins, and for everyone who served on both sides, the War was the most important experience of their lives.

GRANDPA

"Grandpa, what was it like in the War?"
"You should read my day book, George."
"Where is it, Grandpa?"
"I sent it to the government to get more pension."
"Did they give it to you?"
"No."

William Randall was not a story-teller. He remembered places he had been and things he had seen, but the memories were pictures, not words. The words he had learned in school were not enough for the pictures in his mind. And he had neither training nor talent to draw.

Keeping the little day book had been a struggle. There were only six narrow lines for each day. He found a few words to fill most of the lines, but on many days there was nothing special to write, so that's what he wrote: "nothing specel today."

It had become harder to write as the year passed. He was relieved when the entry was written for December 31, 1864. He did not have a book for the new year. He could have used writing paper, but the lack of a book was a good excuse to stop.

His letters home had been a struggle too, and his wife Cynthia had not saved them. He had written fewer letters in the new year. He had felt sick much of the time, always too cold or too hot, and his soul had ached for his family and home.

His grandson's question pushed William's thoughts back to a time he did not like to remember. He struggled to feed his family from a poor hillside farm. The army had promised him a lot of money when he enlisted, much more than he made from farming. No one told him about marching nearly every day, rarely seeing the enemy, wondering if the War would ever end, and wishing he were back home with his family. It had been a bad time.

And yet, when he met other veterans, men from his regiment in the War, they shook hands warmly, sometimes embraced, joked and laughed. They shared something that did not need words. They had survived the War. Many friends had not. And they had won.

A Letter From Home

"Bill, you have a letter."

Mail for the 161st New York Volunteer Infantry Regiment had found its way to Dauphin Island, Alabama, west of the mouth of Mobile Bay. Private William Randall's regiment had been there about a week. They were waiting for orders to march against Confederate forts that defended the city of Mobile.

The Union Army did a lot of waiting. Their wait in camp at Kennerville, Louisiana, on a bit of high ground between Lake Ponchartrain and the Mississippi River, had ended three weeks ago. They rode rail cars to New Orleans, then marched the remaining miles to Lakeport, where they boarded the steamboat *Planter*.

The *Planter* brought them to Dauphin Island, a wind-blown barrier of seashells and white sand between the Gulf of Mexico and Mobile Bay. Marsh grass, shrubs, and some trees grew along the north shore away from the ocean. The western part of the island was wooded. Tents of the Union Army XIII Corps covered the sand around Fort Gaines at the east end of the island, and as far west as William could see.

Twenty miles north, the city of Mobile was still held by the Confederates. The previous summer the Union Army had captured Fort Gaines on Dauphin Island and Fort Morgan across the main ship channel. That allowed the Navy to tighten their blockade, capturing more blockade runners, and cutting off more Confederate war supplies.

The city of Mobile itself was strongly defended. Three lines of entrenchments and concrete forts guarded the western approaches. To the east across seven miles of rivers and marsh were Spanish Fort and Fort Blakely. The Confederate Army knew how to build strong forts, and they had worked a long time on the ones around Mobile.

William Randall and his New York regiment were assigned an area with other units of 3rd Brigade, 1st Division, XIII Corps. Combined strength of the four regiments in 3rd brigade was about 2,100 men. The 29th Illinois, 30th Missouri, 161st New York, and 23rd Wisconsin Regiments had been together in camp and on marches along the Mississippi River, but they had not yet fought together. XIII Corps was the only Union Army corps that did not wear an identifying insignia on their caps. Lucky Thirteen.

There was always a breeze on Dauphin Island. This was William's first winter in the South and he marvelled at the mild weather. At home he would be plowing a field on a fine March day like this. Here he was cleaning his rifle. Salt air turned the least bit of moisture to rust, and sand stuck to everything. But his sergeant did not accept any excuse for a dirty rifle.

When the bugler sounded "Mail Call," sergeants reported to the Chaplain's tent to collect mail for their companies. The thought of a letter from home reminded William that there was more to his life than marching in a sweat-stiffened wool uniform, eating hardtack and too-salty meat, and sleeping on a rubber blanket on the ground. He put down his rifle-cleaning gear when John, his sergeant, gave him the letter.

The handwriting was different from his wife Cynthia's familiar lines. The postmark said Wellsburg, so it was from someone at home. He used the point of his bayonet to open it. It had been written about two weeks ago, February 17, by Cynthia's brother.

> *Dear William,*
> *I regret that I must take pen in hand*
> *to send sad news. Cynthia is unable to write*
> *so she has asked me to send you this letter.*
> *Your daughter, beautiful little Bertha Jane, has*
> *been called to her eternal reward.*

The words struck him hard, like a rifle butt hitting the center of his chest, taking his breath away. This had to be a mistake. He looked again at the back of the letter to make sure it was addressed to him, Private Wm. H. Randall, 161st New York Regt.

It was.

Bertha Jane was just four years old. She was beginning to help her mother with chores and to look after baby Albert. She could not be gone. But there were the words, blurring in his tear-filled eyes: "Your daughter, beautiful little Bertha Jane, has been called to her eternal reward."

His daughter was dead.

The rest of the letter described the child's final illness, his wife's grief, and the funeral. Cynthia used some of his bounty pay to purchase a fine marble stone, which was inscribed with a beautiful poem. The burial service in Dutchtown Cemetery was conducted by the minister who rode out from Wellsburg. A February thaw softened the ground just enough to allow her grave to be dug.

Cynthia's brother wrote what he thought would be comforting words. Bertha Jane was with her beloved Saviour. She was so innocent and beautiful that He had called her home while she was still a little child. Perhaps the words would comfort him, sometime. Now they seemed empty.

William Randall had seen too many of his fellow soldiers dead. Seventeen men from his regiment met violent death at a place called Pleasant Grove near Sabine Cross Roads. General Franklin said that the 161st New York Regiment saved the Army that day, by delaying the enemy advance until other regiments could form the line of battle. Praise from the General did not bring dead soldiers back to life. Some of those men had joined the regiment just a few days before the battle. William had travelled with them from Elmira, New York, in a detachment of new recruits.

Men died in the angry chaos of battle. Some were enemies, some were comrades. It was kill or be killed, and you did what you had to do. After the battle the wounded were taken to hospital. A few returned to the regiment, one or two at a time, bringing news of others who had died, or who were to be sent home without a leg or an eye or a hand. But that was the nature of war. When you enlisted, you had to be ready to shed your blood for your country. Some of William's friends had been killed, and some had been wounded. That was the price of ending the Rebellion and restoring the Union.

Death in battle was how a soldier was supposed to die. It was sudden, and brutal, and honest. Death from chronic diarrhea was slow and filthy. The previous summer in camps along the Mississippi River, William went to funerals nearly every week. After all a man's strength drained into the latrine pits, he went to the hospital, where life itself drained out of him. When his name was read each morning at roll call, someone answered, "He's in the hospital." Then one day the answer was, "He died last night."

Soldiers died in battle and they died of sickness, but why did a child at home have to die? William thought of his dead son Nehemiah. He was just three years old, and he had been gone seven years. William and Cynthia left him behind in the Port Crane Cemetery when they moved down the Susquehanna River to a new farm south of Elmira, New York. Cynthia still mourned for little Nehemiah, her first-born child. People reminded her that she was blessed with other children, and Truman, Ida, Bertha Jane, and Albert did help her forget her grief. But sometimes when William found her alone in the house, he saw tears in her eyes. He knew that she still thought of Nehemiah.

Now Bertha Jane was gone, too, and grief was renewed. What could he do to comfort his poor wife, who was a thousand miles away? And who would comfort him here, in the Army? Through the blur of mourning a dead child, the War continued.

William folded the letter, and put it back in its envelope, and put it in the patched pocket of his trousers. It felt like a burning coal. He resumed cleaning his rifle, but his mind was still on the letter.

John said, "Bill, you'll wear a hole in that thing if you keep rubbing the same spot. What news from home?"

"My daughter died." Saying the words seemed to make them true. His mind fought the words in the letter, but these words were his own. Bertha Jane was truly gone. He would never see his sweet child again.

"Oh, dear Lord, I am sorry. How did it happen?"

William answered with words from the letter, and spoke of his concern for Cynthia. Her mother was helping with the other children. Bertha was named for Cynthia's mother, or rather, her stepmother. She married Cynthia's father after his first wife died, and she raised Cynthia as her own. It was good that she was able to help Cynthia.

William's words dulled the pain of his grief. They made him think of his family, and the other children, and they took his thoughts from the little girl whom he had not seen in a year, and would not see again.

He responded numbly when a bugle called the regiment to battalion drill. He took his place in ranks and obeyed familiar commands without thinking. "Dress right!" "Shoulder arms!" "Forward, March!" But when there was a break, his thoughts leaped home to farm and family, and stayed there until he heard the captain shouting in his face. Then he was back in the glaring afternoon sun with sand under his feet. His thoughts returned to the drill. Finally the command was given, "Dismissed!"

After supper William walked alone near the ocean. The sun was setting behind a line of golden clouds, leaving the sky a deeper blue than he remembered it at home in New York. Was this the same sky he saw at home? The moon looked the same, and the stars were the ones he saw at home. Orion the Hunter was there, followed by the Dog Star. The Big and Little Dippers were there too. But here the North Star was lower in the sky. His mood was even lower.

Would this miserable War ever end? Would the Confederacy ever surrender, or would it be necessary to kill or capture every last Confederate soldier, in every backwater swamp and woodland in the South? His regiment had chased Rebs last autumn along the Mississippi River, with little success. A swamp had a thousand places for a sniper to hide, and a thousand ways for a man to disappear. Would he have to wait two more years until his enlistment ended before he could go home?

His thoughts turned to the coming campaign. Perhaps he would be killed like his cousin Wesley, a casualty at Bull Run, the first big battle of the War. Death would end his grief, but it would make Cynthia's pain even worse. Who would support her and the other children?

Perhaps he would be wounded. It should not be a painful wound that tore through him and left him crippled like his cousin Lyman. But perhaps a hand or arm wound, preferably his left hand like cousin Ellis, who was shot through the wrist in the battle near Antietam Creek, Maryland. Cousin Frederick had been wounded at Gaines Mill, Virginia, grazed on the scalp by a Minié ball. It did not prevent his promotion to lieutenant, but it "left him unfit for further service" when his enlistment expired. One inch lower and he would have been dead. No, a head wound was too risky. A hand wound might be all right, but not a head wound.

William wondered if Bertha Jane's death was his fault. Was God punishing him for swearing, for playing cards, for getting drunk, for noticing the curves of young slave wenches in their ragged clothes? He tried to live as a Christian, but it was hard in the Army camps.

He attended preaching services when he first joined the Army, and prayer meetings in the camps last summer. Despite all the prayers, God allowed the funerals of his friends to continue. When he got a fever and headache that made him think his head would burst, he bargained with God for the pain to go away. It did eventually, in God's good time. But then he was separated from his regiment, and he failed to attend prayer meetings to keep his end of the bargain.

But if he was at fault, why did his little daughter have to die? God must be terribly cruel to deprive a child of life. God allowed men to die horrible deaths in battle. When William remembered his friends dying of chronic diarrhea, he thought he knew how cruel God could be. He wanted to curse God. He wanted to shake his fists at the sky and to scream, "Why, God, why?"

But instead of screaming, he wept, and he pleaded with God. "Make this War end, Lord. Let me go home to Cynthia and the children. How much longer will I have to wait, Lord? How much farther will I have to march? How many more battles will I have to survive? Please help me, Lord. Bring this War to an end, so I can go home."

CIVIL WAR BEGINS

The American Civil War followed decades of debate and compromise, years of bitter argument, and months of tense dispute. The people of the United States of America disagreed about whether and where Negro slavery should be allowed. The election of Abraham Lincoln as President in 1860 was read in the South as a sign that the dispute could not be resolved. Eleven southern states seceded from the national union and set up the Confederate States of America. They organized armed forces to prevent the federal government from enforcing its laws within their borders. At 4:30 a.m. on April 12, 1861, at Charleston, South Carolina, Confederate artillery opened fire on Fort Sumter. U.S. Army troops surrendered after two days of bombardment. The national union was violently broken.

In 1861 newspapers were as full of bad news as they are today, but the actions of southern state governments were remote from the rural counties of western New York. The dispute over Negro slavery did not seem to affect families who lived and farmed in the valleys of the Susquehanna River and its tributaries. Dissolution of the national union was a different matter, however, and it brought uproar to every town. Preachers, politicians, newspaper editors, and tavern loafers spoke out against the southern states. They were called traitors. They must be forced to return to the Union. Fort Sumter must be avenged. The new President called on the states for 75,000 volunteers, and many more than that responded. The State of New York called out the National Guard and authorized new regiments. Companies formed in each town. There were parades. Flags waved. Bands played stirring music. And men enlisted to restore the Union.

William Randall was not an early volunteer for the Union cause. He was no longer a young man, and he had to provide for his wife Cynthia and their young children. He worked his small farm south of Elmira to feed his family.

William Henry Randall and Cynthia Jane Gleason had been married on June 18, 1853, in the town of Union, Broome County, New York, when William was 26 and Cynthia not yet 17. Their first child was born one year later, on June 24, 1854. He was named Nehemiah Randall, like his grandfather, great grandfather, and second great grandfather. Another son followed two years later, August 17, 1856, named for his Uncle Truman Van Armburgh, the husband of William's Aunt Olive.

On December 7, 1857, three-year-old Nehemiah died. He was buried in the cemetery at Port Crane, on the Chenango River. Daughter Ida was born the following autumn, October 8, 1858. The year 1858 also saw a mortgage foreclosure on the Broome County farm where William's grandfather settled in 1833. After 25 years there, the Randalls lost a home, a livelihood, and a family cemetery.

By the summer of 1860, William and Cynthia had moved fifty miles down the Susquehanna River valley to Bradford County, Pennsylvania. There in Athens Township, William bought land and a house. In the 1860 census, his nearest neighbors reported that their real estate was valued at $4,000 and $1,000. William's home was worth just $300. William and Cynthia were on that same little farm the following spring, when the nation went to war.

William's cousins Ellis, Frederick, and Wesley, sons of Uncle Freeman Randall, were among the men who enlisted in the spring of 1861. Ellis went first, to Company D of the 23rd New York Infantry Regiment. Frederick, the youngest brother, joined the 27th Regiment on May 21, 1861, as a Corporal in Company F. After the patriotic excitement of Independence Day, older brother Wesley joined Fred. Wesley enlisted on July 9 and mustered in the 27th Regiment and F Company on July 15. He had little time to learn to be a soldier. On July 21, the 27th New York Regiment fought in the first Battle of Bull Run.

Folks from Washington rode out toward Manassas and the Bull Run battlefield in their carriages, expecting to see a fine spectacle. The brave boys in blue were going to show the rebels that secession was a mistake. Instead, spectators fled back to Washington in panic, with stories of a Union rout. Wesley Randall was among those lost in the battle. At first, people hoped he was captured and imprisoned at Richmond. Later, when his name did not appear on the lists of prisoners, he was presumed to be dead. His body was never identified.

Wesley's brother, Frederick, survived the first Battle of Bull Run and was promoted to Sergeant. One might say that the battle was a "learning experience": Soldiers learned to master fear, exhaustion, thirst, pain, terror, horror, disgust, and death in order to fight. Officers learned to lead men in battle, and to count the wounded, missing, and dead. In both North and South, citizens and political leaders began to learn that victory would not be as easy as they had imagined. And the Randall family began to learn how much the War would cost in worry, pain, and grief.

Other Randall cousins joined other New York regiments in the second and third years of the War. Andrew and Levi enlisted together in Company E of the 90th infantry, Lyman joined the 64th, and cousin John McDaniel was in the 109th. Men as old as William were not yet needed, and Cynthia had borne two more children, Bertha in 1861 and Albert in 1863. A man with family responsibilities was not expected to go. Not yet.

In the Battle of Antietam on September 17, 1862, cousin Ellis Randall was wounded. That battle near the little town of Sharpsburg, Maryland, was the bloodiest day yet in the on-going slaughter, with more that 23,000 young men killed or wounded. Ellis, who was left-handed, lost the use of his left hand. He was discharged the next spring, unable to do any work that needed two good hands.

Then Frederick Randall was discharged. He had been promoted to sergeant, returned to the ranks as a private, then promoted to second lieutenant. He received "a slight head wound" at Gaines Mill, Virginia, which left him "unfit for further service." He was discharged when his two-year enlistment expired in May 1863.

In the summer of 1863, Confederate armies again crossed the Potomac River to invade the North. Panic spread as General Lee's army and Stuart's cavalry invaded Pennsylvania. General Morgan's cavalry rode through Kentucky, crossed the Ohio River, and raided in Indiana and Ohio. Alarms were raised to defend home ground. After the Battle of Gettysburg, Lee's troops retreated to Virginia. Morgan was captured in eastern Ohio and imprisoned in the state penitentiary.

News arrived that the Confederate defenders of Vicksburg, Mississippi, had surrendered after a long siege on July 4, 1863. When Port Hudson, Louisiana, surrendered on July 9th, the Mississippi River was entirely in Union hands.

The Randall family continued to pay the cost of war. Lyman Randall was wounded in October 1863 at Bristoe's Mill, Virginia, by a Minié bullet that passed through his right hip. Surgery in a field hospital did more damage before he was sent to the 3rd Division Hospital in Washington. In January 1864 he was well enough to be granted a thirty-day furlough to return to his home in New York.

WILLIAM RANDALL JOINS THE ARMY
(Jan 23–Mar 27, 1864)

Of the seven young men the Randall family had sent to war, one was dead, three were maimed, and three continued in the struggle. Three more Randall cousins volunteered in 1864. They were attracted by large bounty payments, more money than they could earn from several years of farming. They were also threatened with the draft, and no bounty, if they did not volunteer. William Randall joined in January. Lyman Randall's brothers, West and John, enlisted together in March. West was 36 years old and John was 31. William was 37 and the father of four young children, the oldest only eight years old.

Although William lived south of the state line, it was easier to travel to Elmira, New York, than to any sizeable town in Pennsylvania (as it still is today). Enlistment bounties were higher in New York too.

William joined the 161st New York Volunteer Infantry Regiment on Saturday, January 23, 1864, at Elmira, New York The regiment had been organized at Elmira in 1862. They had not fought in the famous eastern campaigns and battles, but they still needed new men to replace the dead and the discharged. Their ranks were thinned in battles along the Mississippi River at Port Hudson and Cox's Plantation, and by the steady drain of sickness. In January 1864, William signed up with a regiment of veterans.

Seven weeks later, William began to make entries in his day-book, when he arrived in New York City on the way to join his regiment. He travelled with a group of about eighty new soldiers. At New York City they boarded a steamship that took them to New Orleans. Then they spent several days in New Orleans, waiting to be sent on to their regiment. This was the farthest that William had ever travelled from his birthplace in the Susquehanna River valley.

> **THURSDAY, MARCH 10, 1864** *Got into New York about 9 o'clock AM. Got our breakfast in the barracks. We were then marched down to the wharf and on board the boat Varuna. Set sail at 6 PM.*
>
> **FRIDAY 11** *This morning we were out of sight of land. The sea was rough and many of the soldiers were seasick.*
>
> **SATURDAY 12** *This day was fair but the sea rough. Saw one of U.S. gunboats which fired a shot and brought us to [that is, stopped us] till our papers were examined.*
>
> **SUNDAY, MARCH 13, 1864** *This day is very beautiful but the soldiers and sailors hardly seem to know that it is Sunday.*

William expected better behavior than he found among his shipmates. In particular, they showed less respect for the Sabbath than he expected.

> **MONDAY 14** *This day we are making about 12 miles per hour. Some of the soldiers got into a fight on deck and some were tied up till they could behave themselves.*
>
> **TUESDAY 15** *This day is very beautiful. We sail along the eastern coast of Florida. We saw several sails today.*
>
> **WEDNESDAY, MARCH 16, 1864** *This morning fair. Soon came a shark [which] was seen to follow us.*

> **THURSDAY 17** *This morning found us around Cape Florida and about 1 o'clock cast anchor at Key West. Sent a letter home.*
>
> **FRIDAY 18** *Remained here in port today. The boat took in coal and water. At night started for New Orleans.*
>
> **SATURDAY, MARCH 19, 1864** *This forenoon a gunboat followed us till she saw who we were. Then she turned away and was soon out of sight.*
>
> **SUNDAY 20** *This is a beautiful day. We make very good sail. One of the soldiers by the [name] of H. A. Conrad preached on deck.*

March 20 was Palm Sunday, a day of celebration for Christians.

Private Henry A. Conrad, age 41, enlisted at Farmersville, Cattaraugus County, and was assigned to Company D on January 2, 1864. His son Hendrick Conrad, age 18, enlisted with him. Hendrick died of typhoid on September 6, 1864, on the transport Kate Dale in Mobile Bay. He was buried at sea. Henry survived and was mustered out of the Army on June 20, 1865, from a hospital at Alexandria, Virginia.

> **MONDAY 21** *This morning it was rainy. The wind was blowing a gale and the sea very rough. About 3 PM we entered the mouth of the Mississippi. Came up to the quarantine.*
>
> **TUESDAY, MARCH 22, 1864** *This morning found us wet and cold. At 5 PM a steamer took us in tow for New Orleans. It [be]came soft warm in the afternoon so our clothes dried.*
>
> **WEDNESDAY 23** *About 10 AM came up to New Orleans and at 2 o'clock PM were marched to the barracks, which was Factors Cotton Press.*
>
> **THURSDAY 24** *Nothing unusual occurred today, we remaining in the barracks.*
>
> **FRIDAY, MARCH 25, 1864** *The day passed off as usual. At night we had prayer meeting in the mess room.*

March 25 was Good Friday.

> **SATURDAY 26** *Got a pass. Went out into the city. At night had prayer meeting in the mess room.*
>
> **SUNDAY 27** *A man from the Commission Nab[?]us preached to us in the morning and in the afternoon H. A. Conrad preached and at night had prayer meeting.*

This was Easter Sunday.

Along the Red River in Louisiana

MARCH 28–APRIL 7

In the spring of 1864, a Union Army commanded by Major General Nathaniel P. Banks marched from southern Louisiana. They planned to attack Shreveport, where the Confederates had moved the Louisiana state government after Union troops captured Baton Rouge. Union Navy gunboats under Rear Admiral David D. Porter supported Banks's army along the Red River. Another Union Army under Major General Frederick Steele was coming from Little Rock, Arkansas, to join the attack. Union generals planned to invade Texas after Shreveport was captured. Commanders expected large stores of cotton to be seized in the campaign, for sale at high prices to cotton-starved mills in the northern states and England.

Cotton trading interests and political concerns were important factors in the Red River Campaign. New England mill owners desperately needed cotton. General Banks, who was from Massachusetts, wanted their help so he could displace President Abraham Lincoln as the Republican presidential candidate. Cotton trading in the part of the South held by the Union Army was controlled by the U.S. Treasury Department, and Treasury Secretary Salmon P. Chase also had ambitions to be President. Admiral Porter undertook the expedition to gain valuable cotton bales as "naval prizes of war", which would enrich him and his officers and crews. The Republicans needed electoral votes from a "reconstructed" Louisiana state government that was loyal to the Union.

The campaign disappointed everyone except the cotton brokers. Thousands of bales of cotton were burned by both Confederate and Union troops, but a few thousand bales reached New Orleans. There they generated sales commissions, which enriched commercial and Treasury agents and their friends. In 1864, cotton exports from the southern states fell to one-sixth of pre-war levels, and the price rose to six times the pre-war level. President Lincoln complained that, in spite of a trade embargo and blockade of the southern ports, Confederates who were selling cotton had the same amount of wealth as before the War to purchase war supplies.

While it enriched cotton traders, the Red River Campaign turned into a military disaster for General Banks. Confederate units from Texas and Arkansas joined with Louisiana divisions to attack his Union army. Low water in the Red River stranded Admiral Porter's gunboats above the falls at Alexandria. General Banks could not coordinate movements of his army in Louisiana with General Steele in Arkansas. Steele's army was crippled by lack of supplies. The Confederates chased Banks away from Shreveport, then they chased Steele back to Little Rock. Banks's army retreated down the Red River, and he was relieved of command of troops in the field.

General Banks's army on the Red River included a cavalry division, two divisions of XIX Corps, two divisions of XIII Corps, and a brigade of Corps d'Afrique (ex-slaves who had enlisted in the Union Army). Major General William T. Sherman loaned three divisions from XVI and XVII Corps to the campaign. A total of 30,000 men were present for duty. After the campaign began, Private William Randall caught up with Company K of the 161st New York Volunteer Infantry Regiment, which was assigned at that time to First Brigade, First Division, XIX Corps.

The Red River Campaign began on March 10, 1864, when divisions loaned by General Sherman embarked at Vicksburg in steamboats and barges. Union Navy and Army forces entered the Red River on March 12, captured Fort De Russy on the 14th, and occupied Alexandria on the 16th. They were opposed by troops commanded by Confederate Major General Richard Taylor, son of former U.S. President Zachary Taylor and brother-in-law of Confederate President Jefferson Davis. Union cavalry skirmished with Confederate infantry at Marksville, Black Bayou, Bayou Rapides, and Henderson's Hill.

Admiral Porter's gunboats were delayed at Alexandria for several days by low water before they could pass the falls. His sailors used the time to collect more bales of cotton.

General Banks followed with the rest of his army. The troops under his direct control did not leave Franklin, Louisiana, until March 15. Hard marching brought them to Alexandria on March 25, where they rested for two days, then moved up the river on March 28. His cavalry continued to skirmish with Confederate infantry: twice at Campti, twice at Natchitoches, and at Monett's Ferry, Cloutierville, Crump's Hill, and Grand Ecore.

William Randall reached his regiment on April 4, north of Alexandria near Grand Ecore. When he arrived they had been campaigning for more than three weeks.

They had not yet engaged Confederate troops but they had marched through hail, rainstorms, and mud before he arrived on a steamboat from New Orleans.

> **MONDAY, MARCH 28, 1864** *Left New Orleans about eight o'clock in the morning.*
>
> **TUESDAY 29** *This morning finds us sailing up the Mississippi. We see on each side nice plantations and a great many sugar mills but no school houses.*

As he looked for school houses, William thought of his children at home. These sugar and cotton plantations with their rich mansions were not like the modest farms of the Susquehanna River valley, or the home of his family in Athens Township.

> **WEDNESDAY 30** *Today we enter the Red River. See a lot of alligators.*
>
> **THURSDAY, MARCH 31, 1864** *Came up to Alexandria. Here a lot of Reb cavalry came in and gave themselves up. Tired of the Rebellion.*
>
> **FRIDAY, APRIL 1** *About noon we left Alexandria, and in the afternoon came up with the fleet sent to reinforce Banks. Stayed here all night.*
>
> **SATURDAY 2** *Started out in the afternoon, but soon tied up for the night.*
>
> **SUNDAY, APRIL 3, 1864** *Today came up to Grand Ecore. Here we lay the remainder of the day and all night.*
>
> **MONDAY 4** *Left the boat about ten o'clock in the morning. Got to the regiment about one o'clock in the afternoon.*

The soldiers who travelled with William Randall were the second group of "fresh fish" to join the regiment in less than a month. An earlier group of 76 new recruits arrived on March 14 with First Lieutenant Royal R. Soper.

> **TUESDAY 5** *Today we laid in camp. This is a beautiful place. Cypress, gum trees, and oak grows here, also grape in abundance.*

Private John W. Merwin's *Monograph and Roster* of 161st Regiment also praised the camp near Natchitoches, Louisiana:

> We have a fine camp about half a mile outside the town in the midst of a beautiful wood free from underbrush, good sward [that is, grass], and a good stream of water near by....This is one of the oldest towns in the United States, being settled by the Spaniards nearly 200 years ago. There are some fairly good dwellings, but the streets are very narrow and before the War had a population of about 4,000. The most notable feature here is the large convent situated on a high bluff overlooking the

town. Many of our men have gone up there and have been courteously received and shown through the building by the Mother Superior.

Private George C. Coleman wrote to his parents from Natchitoches on April 4th, 1864:

The country this side of Alexandria is more rolling than any of Louisiana we have seen heretofore. It is a relief to once more see stones cropping from the hillside and now and then a gliding stream rippling over a pebbley [sic] bottom. We came twelve miles through pine woods which is the only pine I believe I have seen in the state to amount to anything.

Spring in Louisiana impressed other soldiers, too. A year before, Sergeant Lewis E. Fitch had praised the climate. In a letter from Baton Rouge, April 4, 1863, he wrote to his brother: "Trees are in full leaf, roses in bloom, onions, radishes and other vegetables large enough to eat, and have been for some time. Day, very warm, and nights, cool."

In a second letter from Baton Rouge, April 25, 1863, Fitch wrote to his friend Charles Fairman:

Though it is yet early in the season the sun shines with all the force of mid-summer farther north, and garden vegetables, young potatoes, peas, radishes, etc., abound, testifying to the difference of latitude. For the comfort of the men we have been supplied with straw hats and musketo [sic] bars, indeed it is almost impossible to rest at night without them, for all can testify they are a most ravenous and bloodthirsty little foe.

William Randall and the other new recruits soon learned what the veterans knew too well: There was more to spring in Louisiana than pleasant camps, warm weather, and mosquitos. It was a time for marching and fighting, too.

> **WEDNESDAY, APRIL 6, 1864** *Started on the first march for thirty miles. March sixteen miles and camped in a low beach flat. The water is the best I [have] seen.*

On April 6 General Banks's army moved northwest from Natchitoches and Grand Ecore, pursuing the defenders toward Shreveport. Union officers believed there were Confederate gunboats and rams on the Red River, obstructions in it, and guns along its banks, all of which would prevent free passage of their fleet. General Banks thought he had to move away from the river, where he could have been supplied by transports and supported by Admiral Porter's gunboats. The road he chose passed through the "piney woods," a pitch pine forest with only a few clearings for small

plantations, and with no forage for troops and horses before reaching Pleasant Hill and Mansfield. The Union troops were accompanied by two long wagon trains of supplies.

> **THURSDAY 7** *Marched 18 miles and camped on Pleasant Hill. We had a smart shower.*

General Banks's cavalry fought another skirmish at Wilson's Plantation near Pleasant Hill on April 7. This time they had to drive back a force of Confederate cavalry instead of a few foot soldiers. The Confederates were being reinforced by troops from Texas. But General Banks and his officers did not understand how the situation was changing.

A HARD FIGHT AT PLEASANT GROVE
(April 8)

The next day, April 8, 1864, the road through the piney woods of northwest Louisiana was muddy and almost impassable. General Banks's Union army was stretched along it for many miles. The leading cavalry division was followed by its artillery and a train of 300 supply wagons. Then came two infantry divisions of XIII Corps, one infantry division of XIX Corps, and a longer train of 700 wagons.

Fifteen miles northwest of Pleasant Hill and three miles south of Mansfield is a place called Sabine Cross-Roads. Confederate units from Texas and Arkansas had arrived there to reinforce the Louisiana troops who had been skirmishing against Union cavalry along the Red River through the past three weeks. Confederate General Taylor deployed his newly-strengthened army on both sides of the road, on a hill commanding the Union approach from the south. Confederate troops were hidden in the edge of dense woods with an open field in front of them. It was a well-placed trap, and the Union Army came right into it.

When the Union cavalry division and leading infantry division finally saw General Taylor's army, they tried to form a line of battle. The Confederate attack quickly outflanked them and routed them. It occurred to General Banks that this was to be more than another cavalry skirmish, so he ordered his trailing infantry divisions to advance rapidly along the muddy road. The next Union infantry division ran into fleeing troops, horses, and supply wagons, but they were able to form a line that held the Confederates for an hour.

Next along the road was First Brigade, First Division, XIX Corps, commanded by Brigadier General William Dwight. They had marched from Pleasant Hill in the morning and set up camp beyond a saw-mill on the Mansfield Road. Sergeant Joseph B. Davidson wrote later of this day for the *Elmira Daily Advertiser*:

Resuming our march again in the morning at daylight, the music of
Nims' battery [that is, the sound of cannons] at the front announced that
the enemy were again disputing the advance. We halted several times
during the forenoon, until the advance had cleared the road and woods
of the enemy. Finally, at 2 o'clock, P.M. the Nineteenth Corps was filed
off the road, and, as was supposed, went into camp for the night. We
did not rest long in this position. The continued and rapid discharge of
artillery, away some six miles to the front, indicated the progress of a
heavy fight, and such proved to be the case.

Now they moved in double-quick time to a place called Pleasant Grove.

General Dwight wrote of the action in his official report:

At about 3 p.m. orders were received from the division commander to
get in readiness to move to the front, with canteens filled with water, and
hard bread, coffee, and sugar for two days. [The 161st New York Infantry
Regiment was at the head of Dwight's Brigade.] As the brigade proceeded
on this march, the firing in the front became heavier, and the rumors from
the field were of disaster, and indicated that the presence of the command
was necessary. Its march was hastened in consequence. Soon fugitives
from the field appeared, consisting, at first, principally of negroes with
spare horses, followed by cavalrymen and wagons. Acting on instructions
from the brigadier-general commanding the division [William H.
Emory], these fugitives were checked and turned back, but their number
continuing to increase, two companies from the One hundred and sixty-
first New York Volunteers were marched in line of battle on each side of
the column. In this order the command reached the top of a hill, where it
met the whole of that portion of the army which had preceded it, in utter
rout and panic, flying before the enemy, who were in hot pursuit.

General Emory ordered his division to form a line of battle in a clearing on the
crest of the hill. He personally led the 161st New York Regiment forward to the edge
of the clearing, to a position in front of the main line. Four companies moved ahead
as skirmishers. There they slowed the enemy, to allow deployment of the rest of the
division, before they were pushed back. Lieutenant John F. Little wrote of the fight
to the editor of the Bath, New York, *Steuben Farmers Advocate*:

After being under a murderous fire of musketry for thirty-five minutes,
we were withdrawn from the advance and fell in with the regiment on
the proper line of battle. The skirmishers being out flanked on the right,
and having used up their ammunition, (40 rounds), were rallied and
moved off the field and joined the battalion.

General Dwight placed the remaining three regiments of his brigade,

> stretching across the road upon which the routed army was passing. After being posted, these regiments were directed to remain firmly in their positions, to reserve their fire until the last moment, and to fire as low as possible. The first attack of the enemy was made upon the front of this line and was repulsed by its steady and withering fire.

Private Merwin also recalled the action:

> When the division line was formed the [161st] regiment was ordered to retire and reform in rear of the line and resume its proper position. As it began to fall back the rebels came out with a yell and tried to take them in, but were not able; but they were right in amongst the men and it was hand to hand for a few moments. In fact they were mixed with us to such an extent that the 29th Maine holding the Mansfield road, fired a volley and a number of our men were hit by the bullets of our friends.

General Dwight sensed that the attack was shifting to his right flank. There he found a great confusion of troops from the three Union divisions that had been ahead of him on the road:

> I endeavored to rally the men on my right, and to move them on to the line of battle, when a few shots from the enemy falling among them, they began to fire wildly in the air and to fall back. After a few moments they became calmer, a portion of them moved up to the line of battle, and by this time order seemed to be restored on the right of the brigade. I immediately went to the left of the brigade. I found the One hundred and sixty-first New York Volunteers, which had retired from in front of the brigade line of battle, formed in the rear of the Twenty-ninth Maine Volunteers, and I directed it to the right of the line to render that secure against further disorder.

The Confederate units were also in disorder. They had hotly chased the Yankees for three miles. They had overrun the Union supply trains and artillery. They were running out of steam and they could not sustain the attack any longer. They had captured 2,500 Union prisoners, 250 supply wagons, and 20 cannons and ammunition. They soon put the captured artillery to use against its former owners.

Company K, 161st New York Regiment, lost eleven men in the fight at Pleasant Grove. Three men were killed:

- **Corporal Frederick O. Brookins** was first reported missing, then determined to be dead.

- **Private Carr Evans** was first reported wounded but he soon died.
- **Private William Watkins** was first reported missing, then determined to be dead.

Six men were wounded:

- **Captain George M. Tillson**, company commander, age 23 years, was wounded in his right arm, which had to be amputated. He would be honorably discharged on September 16, 1864, because of disability.
- **Private Joseph Budd** was wounded in the leg.
- **Private George Grant** was wounded in the leg. He was also captured.
- **Private John Lloyd** was wounded in the thigh.
- **Private Leonard M. Russell** had a head wound. He would die on May 7 in New Orleans.
- **Private Thomas T. Smith** was wounded in the left hand.

In addition to George Grant, Privates Horace N. Brown and William Wilson were captured. Grant would be released in June. The others were not released until October.

Privates Watkins, Russell, and Smith were among the new recruits who had just joined the company. Others from the regiment who were lost included George C. Coleman and Lewis E. Fitch. Private Coleman was first reported to be wounded in the right hip and leg, but he soon died. Lieutenant Fitch, who had recently been promoted from Sergeant, was missing. It was learned later that he was among the dead. The 161st Regiment lost 17 men killed, 41 wounded, and 29 missing — a total of 87 men — at the place called Pleasant Grove.

A BATTLE AT PLEASANT HILL
(April 9)

The Battle of Sabine Cross Roads, Louisiana, also called the Battle of Mansfield, was Private William Randall's first experience in combat. It was followed the next day by the Battle of Pleasant Hill. This is what William wrote in his day book about the two battles:

> **FRIDAY 8** *We marched 12 miles and camped 4 hours and then we marched 8 miles and went in a hard fight.*
>
> **SATURDAY, APRIL 9, 1864** *Then we retired back to Pleasant Hill about 20 miles and formed a line of battle about 10 o'clock. Ended at dark. Took 226 prisoners.*

The *Official Record* and newspaper accounts give more detail. General William Dwight's report of the actions of First Brigade, First Division, XIX Corps, during the night of April 8-9, states this:

> After firing had ceased [at Pleasant Grove] strong pickets were thrown to the front of this brigade, and many prisoners were taken by them. They were carefully directed on no account to fire, but to use all their exertions to capture. In the stillness of evening which followed nothing was to be heard at first but the groans of the wounded and dying in front of this position, mingled with the shouts of the enemy over the spoils found in the wagons which they had captured. These sounds were followed by the rumbling of wagons going to the enemy's rear. Mean time my pickets and the prisoners they captured gave accurate information of the movements of the enemy's infantry and cavalry, all of which indicated that the position was to be attacked at early dawn. Between 9 and 10 p.m. I was informed of the intention to retire the army to Pleasant Hill, and at the same time the brigadier-general commanding the division [William H. Emory] charged this brigade with the duty of bringing up the rear. As the brigade pickets were within a few feet of those of the enemy, to do this without his knowledge was a difficult operation. I sent for the commanding officers of the different regiments and gave them the most minute instructions as to the proceeding.

The army had to retreat from Pleasant Grove because there was no water there for exhausted soldiers and horses. Around midnight, General Dwight's troops slipped silently back from their enemy and withdrew on the road to Pleasant Hill. He wrote, "This march to Pleasant Hill was a painful one, as many delays were caused, owing to the long wagon trains and great number of stragglers along the road...." They reached Pleasant Hill at 7 a.m., with Confederate cavalry starting to skirmish with their rear guard.

It was a cold, sour Saturday morning. A *New York Tribune* reporter wrote,

> The wind howled piteously through the trees, fanning the long pendants of gray, funeral like moss which decked the tops of the tall waving cypress and pines. The sky was shrouded with portentous clouds, while dense volumes of dust partially concealed the long pontoon trains as they rumbled heavily to the rear.

The reporter described the battlefield at Pleasant Hill as.

> a large, open field, which had once been cultivated, but is now overgrown with weeds and bushes. The slightly elevated centre of the field, from which the name Pleasant Hill is taken, is nothing more than

a long mound, hardly worth the name of a hill. A semicircular belt of timber runs around the field on the Shreveport side.

General Dwight's official report did not mention weather or geography.

> On arriving at Pleasant Hill this brigade took, by direction of the brigadier-general commanding the division, the same ground which it had left the previous morning, having accomplished in twenty-four hours 40 miles of marching, much severe fighting, and a delicate retirement in the face of the enemy. When this brigade thus took up its old ground a large body of troops, supposed to be under the command of Brig. Gen. A. J. Smith, were between it and the enemy. It was therefore permitted to rest and to cook. The wagons belonging to the brigade were, by direction of the brigadier-general commanding the division, sent to the rear. There was a good deal of picket firing during the day, which between 4 and 5 o'clock became frequent, and at moments heavy, and I directed that the brigade should stand to its arms.

General Banks's report described the setting and the start of the battle:

> Pleasant Hill represents a plain about 1 mile square, the residences of the town being located upon its borders. It has a gentle slope to the west. Surrounding it were extensive tracts of woodland.... The enemy began to reconnoiter the new position we had assumed at 11 o'clock on the morning of the 9th, and as early as 1 or 2 o'clock opened a sharp fire of skirmishers, which was kept up at intervals during the afternoon.... Skirmishing continued during the afternoon with occasional discharges of artillery.

General Banks did not report his instructions about how the army was to be deployed for the approaching battle. General Emory formed his division into line of battle facing the woods from which the Confederates were expected to attack. General McMillan's brigade was on the right, General Dwight's brigade (including the 161st Regiment) was in the center, and Colonel Benedict's brigade was on the left. One brigade from General A. J. Smith's two divisions was between General Dwight's brigade and the woods. Other brigades of Smith's divisions were behind Benedict's brigade, out of sight of the Confederates. The *New York Tribune* reported,

> In the rear of Emory, and concealed by the rising ground were Gen. Smith's tired troops, formed in two lines of battle fifty yards apart. [They were tired because they had marched all night.] All his artillery was in the front line, a piece, section or battery being on the flank of each regiment, the infantry lying between them.

Around 4:15 p.m. Confederate cavalry moved against the right and center of the Union lines. At 5 p.m. a more powerful infantry attack was launched against the Union left. The Confederates pushed back the Union troops in several places. As Colonel Benedict's brigade gave way, they slipped through General Smith's lines.

The *New York Tribune* reported the turn of the battle. The Confederates approached in two lines.

> The first passed over the knoll, and all heedless of the long line of cannons and crouching forms of as brave men as ever trod mother earth, pressed on. The second line appeared on the crest, and the death signal was sounded. Words cannot describe the awful effect of this discharge. Seven thousand rifles, and several batteries of artillery, each gun loaded to the muzzle with grape and canister, were fired simultaneously, and the whole center of the Rebel line was crushed down as a field of ripe wheat through which a tornado had passed. It is estimated that 1,000 men were hurried into eternity or frightfully mangled by this one discharge.
>
> No time was given them to recover their good order, but General Smith ordered a charge, and his men dashed rapidly forward.... The Rebels fought boldly and desperately back to the timber, on reaching which a large portion broke and fled, fully two thousand throwing aside their arms. In this charge Taylor's battery was retaken, as were also two of the guns of Nims's Battery, the Parrott gun taken from us at Carrion Crow last fall, and one or two others belonging to the Rebels, one of which was considerably shattered, besides 700 prisoners. A pursuit and desultory fight was kept up for three miles, when our men returned to the field of battle.

As the action proceeded, General Dwight found Confederate troops in his rear, along the road connecting him with his division commander.

> I directed the one hundred and sixty-first New York Volunteers, Lieutenant-Colonel Kinsey, to move in column of companies upon the road to clear it of the enemy, if necessary with the bayonet. This movement was executed with promptness. The officers, and particularly Lieutenant-Colonel Kinsey, who commanded, are deserving of special praise and mention.

Early newspaper reports of the battles of April 8 and 9 gave credit to General A. J. Smith and troops of his XVI Corps for saving General Banks's army and for the victory at Pleasant Hill. Later reports gave more accurate accounts. On July 1, 1864, the *Elmira Daily Advertiser* published a letter to the editor from Sergeant Joseph B.

Davidson, written from Morganza Bend, Louisiana, on June 6. Davidson wrote,

> Thus the contest raged until sundown when they were driven from the field, leaving their dead and wounded; their attack on our left and centre failed with terrible loss. Massing their forces they made an impetuous assault on our right. Here they were met by the 1st Brigade of the Nineteenth Corps which had punished and repulsed them the day before at Mansfield. They met the same fate here after half an hour's fighting with musketry, fleeing in disorder and leaving our victory complete. Thus was the battle won — not by a single corps as has been reported, but by the valiant conduct of all engaged....

Sergeant Davidson added,

> The 161st was more fortunate here than at Mansfield. This with the fact that they were a well drilled regiment induced Gen. Emory to hold them as a reserve to be moved to any part of the field where there was danger of our line being broken and support needed. We were kept on the move at double-quick much of the time. Col. Kinsey himself on foot, having had both his horses killed under him at Mansfield, would barely get his regiment formed before he would get orders to move them to another position. All did their duty with faithfulness and bravery.

RETREAT AFTER VICTORY
(April 10–29)

In his official report of the Battle of Pleasant Hill, General Banks wrote that Confederate casualties were more than twice the losses among his army, that the losses among Confederate officers were said to be very great, that some of the cannons lost the day before were recaptured, that his troops captured a large number of small arms and 500 prisoners, that the rout of the enemy was complete. Nevertheless, his victorious army had to withdraw instead of pursuing the defeated enemy because he had sent his supplies far to the rear. There was no water and no food for troops or horses after a warm day and a hot battle. The "victorious" Union army retreated to Grand Ecore, pursued by the "routed" Confederates.

William Randall wrote in his day book about the retreat.

> **SUNDAY 10** *We marched all day. Tired and paraded out. Camped on the same ground where we camped from Natchitoches on the first day we marched.*

> **MONDAY 11** *We march back to the shore to Grand Ecore on bluff of the river and camp near the road.*

Sergeant Joseph B. Davidson continued, in his letter to the editor of the *Elmira Daily Advertiser*,

> After we had fallen back to Grand Ecore the 161st was called into line by Brigadier General Dwight for the purpose of conveying the thanks of Gens. Franklin and Emory to the commander and men of the 161st for their valuable services at Mansfield. Gen. Dwight stated that he was authorized by Generals Franklin and Emory to say to the 161st that their good conduct at Mansfield saved the whole Army of the Gulf from destruction. They said they had seen much fighting, and experienced many reverses, but they assured us that they never saw anything so perfectly terrifying as was the condition of things at Mansfield at the time of the arrival of the 161st.

TUESDAY, APRIL 12, 1864 *We are in camp. The news was that the rebels had blockaded the river to keep our boats up there so [as] to starve us out.*

WEDNESDAY 13 *Cannonading all day in distant hearing. They drove them back and come down the river some slivered up.*

Admiral Porter had taken his gunboats and the army's transports up the Red River from Grand Ecore on April 7. After the Battle of Pleasant Hill, General Taylor sent Confederate cavalry units with artillery to cut him off. There were several engagements on the 12th and 13th. The gunboats and transports returned to Grand Ecore, damaged by Confederate shells and the shallow river.

THURSDAY 14 *We are in camp. The rebels drove our pickets in.*

FRIDAY, APRIL 15, 1864 *We commenced fortifying today. Avery fined and [assigned extra] duty. Quite a stir.*

"Avery" was Private Benjamin F. Avery of Company D, age 18, who enlisted at Owego, Tioga County, on February 8, 1864. He had travelled with William's cohort to join the regiment. Three other men named Avery enlisted in Company I at Cohocton in August, 1862, but only Corporal Gilbert F. Avery survived. Sergeant Edwin C. Avery, age 24, died at New York City on November 30, 1862. Private John A. Avery, age 19, died at New Orleans on June 1, 1863. Both men died in hospital. The cause of the stir and of Avery's punishment are not known.

SATURDAY 16 *We are in camp. I helped unload boats.*

SUNDAY 17 *We are in camp. Nothing special going on. We had meeting this evening.*

William recorded his attendance at prayer meetings, which provided the comforting assurance that God was present, even in the midst of war.

MONDAY, APRIL 18, 1864 *We were called out on picket. Stayed all night on post.*

TUESDAY 19 *We stayed till three o'clock PM then went to camp.*

WEDNESDAY 20 *We expected to be called out today but we are here yet. The Sixteen Army Corps is called out.*

THURSDAY, APRIL 21, 1864 *We are ordered out in a line ready to start. We laid down till half past 12 o'clock.*

The Union army fortified their position at Grand Ecore. On April 16 General Banks received a sharp reminder from General Sherman that Sherman's troops were needed in Tennessee, and that they should have returned by April 10. Withdrawal of Sherman's three divisions would reduce Banks's army to only 20,000 men, whom he believed to be outnumbered by the Confederate force opposing him. He also believed that the Confederates would "defend Shreveport to the last extremity." He sent a message to Lieutenant General Ulysses S. Grant, newly appointed Commanding General of the U.S. Army, asking for reinforcements.

In fact, the Confederate army facing General Banks was quite small. At Pleasant Hill, Banks had 12,000 Union troops against General Taylor's Confederate force of about the same size. (Banks had left divisions at Alexandria and at Grand Ecore, and the three divisions routed at Sabine Cross Roads were not available.) After the Battle of Pleasant Hill, Confederate Lieutenant General E. Kirby Smith, who commanded the Trans-Mississippi Department, sent three infantry divisions north to oppose General Steele's army in Arkansas. Taylor was left with 4,000 cavalrymen and one infantry division of 2,000 men. They harassed Banks's much larger army and chased him from the Red River.

No reinforcements were available for General Banks, and Admiral Porter was concerned that his boats would be stranded by falling water levels in the river. It was necessary for the Union forces to retreat from Grand Ecore to Alexandria. They moved on April 21 and 22. On April 23, they met and defeated Confederate troops on the bluff above Monett's Ferry on the Cane River, south of Natchitoches. William Randall heard the fight, but the Official Record has no report of his regiment being engaged. Private John Merwin and Chaplain William E. Jones both wrote that 161st New York Regiment moved through a swamp in waist-deep water to provide covering fire while other regiments attacked.

FRIDAY 22 *We started out 1 o'clock PM, and march all day till 12 o'clock PM and camped on Cane River. Went 40 miles.*

SATURDAY 23 *We on [the march] about 9 o'clock AM. March 8 miles and the firing commenced. Kept up all day till almost sundown. They skedaddled. We took 2000 prisoners. Camp 5 miles ahead.*

SUNDAY, APRIL 24, 1864 *We started about 7 o'clock AM. Come out on the Red River and rested 2 hours and camped up by the bayou at sundown.*

MONDAY 25 *We commenced to march about 6 o'clock AM, and got in camp to Alexandria just before sundown. I [am] tired out.*

TUESDAY 26 *I am quite ill and very weak today. Very hot. Good news from General Smith [who] has captured a lot [of] rebels.*

Brigadier General Andrew Jackson Smith commanded two divisions loaned by General Sherman from XVI Corps. His troops were assigned as the rear guard of General Banks's retreating army. They looted and burned and left nothing of value behind. They acted from an inclination to vandalism, from a desire for revenge against rebels and sympathizers, from the habits of their hard war experience, and under command of their officers. General Banks disapproved of their actions but he did not stop them. In later campaigns, in Georgia and the Carolinas, General Sherman's army followed a similar practice of looting and burning property of civilians. Sherman's policy was to punish those who were disloyal to the Union and sympathetic to the Confederacy, but it was not always possible to determine who was loyal to the Union before fire destroyed a home.

WEDNESDAY, APRIL 27, 1864 *I feel a little better today. Flien reports we are going out tomorrow. It is very warm and hot.*

The identity of "Flien" is unknown. There was no one in the regiment in 1864 with a name that William might have spelled "Flien."

THURSDAY 28 *I feel a little better today. Went out on picket. Come in and pick up our tarps and march over the bayou.*

FRIDAY 29 *We are ordered out in line of battle. Stack arms. Rested a while and were ordered to camp for a month or two.*

SAVING THE NAVY
(April 30–May 22)

The Union army of General Nathaniel P. Banks was encamped near the Red River at Alexandria, Louisiana. They had fought several skirmishes and three battles with Confederate troops commanded by General Richard Taylor. The Union army outnumbered Taylor's force by more than three to one, but General Banks and his officers thought they faced an army of roughly equal strength.

A fleet of Union gunboats under the command of Rear Admiral David D. Porter accompanied General Banks's army. They guarded transports that carried supplies, mail, and men. Confederate cavalry with light artillery moved along the river to harass the Union transports.

There were two rapids or "falls" in the Red River at Alexandria, where the river fell more than seven feet over two rocky ledges. Admiral Porter's gunboats had been delayed there on the trip upstream, but they had been able to pass in high water. Now, the water level had dropped. Shallow draft transports could still pass, but the gunboats could not. They were trapped above the rapids until the river rose again, which would probably not be for several months.

The Mississippi River was rising while the Red River was falling. There had been little rain in western Louisiana in April. Veteran steamboat men who knew the Red River had never seen it so low on April 30. The Confederates were reported to have made a canal or cut-off above Grand Ecore, which diverted some of the flow into Grand Lake. But Grand Lake was drained by Grand Bayou and Bayou Pierre, which flowed back into the Red River above Alexandria. There was disagreement about whether a cut-off into Grand Lake was the cause, but regardless, the water level at Alexandria was too low for Union gunboats to pass the falls.

Lieutenant Colonel Joseph Bailey proposed that dams be constructed at the falls, to restrict the flow and deepen a path of water through which boats could pass. Admiral Porter said it would not work, but General Banks told Bailey to proceed. Using materials that were close at hand, a wooden dam was built from the left (north) bank of the river, and a dam of stone-filled barges was built from the right bank. Colonel Bailey reported that at the place where the main dams were constructed, the river was 758 feet wide with a 4 to 6 foot depth of water and a current of about 10 miles per hour.

Several army regiments were put to work on the dams. Most of the army went on reduced rations as supplies became short, but troops working on the dams received extra rations for the hard physical labor. After the troops had worked for nine days and nights, two stone-filled barges broke loose. Five gunboats were able to pass the falls, then two more tried and became stuck. Additional wing dams were built out from shore above the main dams to increase the depth of water. Another dam was built close to the grounded boats, which raised the water level enough to float them free. Then the last three boats, from which cotton cargo and armor and guns had been removed, were finally able to pass. Lieutenant Colonel Bailey was voted the thanks of Congress for saving Admiral Porter's fleet.

The official report of Lieutenant Colonel Uri B. Pearsall states that 161st New York Regiment worked on the river's left bank through the whole period of construction. William Randall's day book states that his company did not join the work until the wing dams were started.

Rear Admiral DAVID D. PORTER

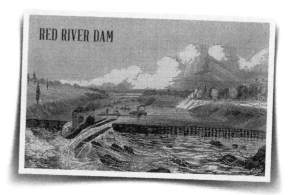
RED RIVER DAM

RED RIVER SHIPS

USS ESSEX

SATURDAY, APRIL 30, 1864 *We were called out and mustered for pay. They commenced damming the river to get the gunboats over the bar.*

SUNDAY, MAY 1 *All quiet and peaceable and lovely today. Very warm indeed. Out on inspection and a very good meeting.*

MONDAY 2 *Went out foraging and made a very good trip but I was very tired. Almost out.*

Food for horses and mules was gathered from the surrounding countryside and from nearby farms. Soldiers also tried to supplement their own rations with what they could find nearby. William was still suffering from the illness and fever that he recorded last week.

TUESDAY, MAY 3, 1864 *This morning we were called out before daylight in a line of battle. Stood about two hours and then ordered back to camp.*

WEDNESDAY 4 *This day of our Lord 1864 called out on drill. The Rebels fired on our pickets with heavy artillery. Fine weather now.*

THURSDAY 5 *Went out and drilled in the morning and on dress parade at night and meeting after dark.*

FRIDAY, MAY 6, 1864 *Company drilled this morning, squad drill at night and meeting after dark.*

SATURDAY 7 *The brigade on fatigue [duty] building breastworks. The cooks went out foraging. Got a hog and some sugar.*

SUNDAY 8 *We are called out on company inspection, at night on brigade inspection. Went to church at 10 o'clock and to the cheleon [?] at night.*

The meaning of "the cheleon" is unknown. William wrote the word clearly in his day book, but his meaning is a mystery.

MONDAY, MAY 9, 1864 *Went out on fatigue [duty], two of us to the commissary store loading up the wagon train and the rest of the company went up on the river [to] work on the dam.*

TUESDAY 10 *The brigade is called out to work on the dam. They shifted the dam. Work all day and all night through. It rained last night.*

WEDNESDAY 11 *We work on the dam. Work all day and all night. The boys got canned beef.*

THURSDAY, MAY 12, 1864 *We are to work on the dam till 8 o'clock PM and then we are ordered back to camp. After dark the order came to tear down and pack up.*

With Admiral Porter's gunboats free and steaming down the river, General Banks's Union army resumed their retreat. General Smith's troops burned the city of Alexandria as they departed.

General Taylor's small Confederate force continued to press the Union army. There were skirmishes at Wilson's Landing on the 14th and on Avoyelles Prairie near Marksville on the 15th. At Mansura on the 16th, Taylor began an artillery duel in a picturesque battle setting. Outnumbered three to one, he withdrew when Union infantry advanced. There was a skirmish at Moreauville on the 17th. On May 18 in the final action of the Red River Campaign, General Smith's rear guard fought Taylor's troops in the woods at Yellow Bayou.

FRIDAY 13 *At 6 o'clock AM we are ordered out in a line to march. We started about 9 AM. Camp near the sugar house just at dark.*

SATURDAY 14 *Called out to march at 3 AM. Skirmishing all day. Camp at dark. Camp on the bank of the river.*

SUNDAY, MAY 15, 1864 *Called in line of march. Ground arms for two hours then left the river. March through the woods and the haul train. In a line of battle and a smart fight at night.*

MONDAY 16 *Called up in a line of battle 4 AM and march in battle 6 miles and then they skedaddle. Then we march across the Bayou Delane, the fight at Marksville.*

TUESDAY 17 *Called out to march down the Bayou Daleese. Camp in 1 mile of the River Chaplio. The rebs fired on the cattle train. Killed 1 man, 3 mules, 1 horse.*

The Official Record states that William's Bayous "Delane" and "Daleese" were Bayou De Glaize. The fight on May 16 was at Mansura. River "Chaplio" was the Atchafalaya.

WEDNESDAY, MAY 18, 1864 *Got a letter from home. Laid in camp all day. General Smith has fought all day in our rear. Drove the rebels and took some prisoners.*

THURSDAY 19 *We march to the river and crossed on the steamboat and marched up the river three miles and camp in a corn field near the river bank.*

Colonel Bailey again demonstrated his ingenuity at the broad Atchafalaya River. All the Union transports were anchored side by side, with planks spanning the narrow gaps. They formed an unusual bridge on which troops and wagon trains could cross safely.

FRIDAY 20 *Laid in camp all day. Just at night the boats started out. Then we were ordered to march just at dark. March till 12 o'clock.*

SATURDAY, MAY 21, 1864 *Camp on the bayou. Started out in the morning. March down the old river a little then down a bayou then we come on the Mississippi then camp.*

SUNDAY 22 *Started on a march down the river 3 miles, then camped on the river bank. Got 6 letters from home.*

With the Red River Campaign ended, General Sherman's three divisions returned to his Army of the Tennessee. In July, the First and Second Divisions of XIX Corps were transferred east where they fought in the Shenandoah Valley Campaign. The 161st New York Regiment stayed in Louisiana.

Public criticism of General Banks was very sharp for the failure of his Red River Campaign. On May 9, this was published in the *New York Times*:

> The business of the General in command at New-Orleans is, in our opinion, to keep possession of the city, to keep the river open up as far as Memphis, and to extend protection to the colonies which we have established along its banks, and then to forward any troops which can be spared from these duties to keep Forrest out of Kentucky, or else to reinforce Sherman. This programme ought to have been rigidly adhered to ever since Vicksburg fell. If it had we should have saved ten or twelve thousand men and many millions worth of stores, and have avoided several humiliating disasters. Surely we have had enough "raids" and "expeditions." Surely their folly has been often enough demonstrated — so often that the repetition of them now falls little short of wickedness.

Major General Edward R. S. Canby relieved General Banks on May 20th. Banks retained command of the Union Army's Department of the Gulf, but he was subordinate to Canby as part of the Military Division of West Mississippi. President

Lincoln found Banks to be a useful political general in the reconstructed government of Louisiana, but the Red River Campaign showed the limits of his talent for military generalship. In dispatches to newspapers and in testimony before the Congressional Committee on the Conduct of the War, Admiral Porter destroyed Banks's public reputation and unfairly assassinated his character. Admiral Porter covered his own cotton dealing, and his own poor judgment about where he could take Navy gunboats, by using a well-known naval tactic: Lay a smoke screen and steam elsewhere.

The Red River and Arkansas Campaigns together cost the Union 8,200 men killed, wounded, and missing in battle. The Union also lost at least 800 wagons loaded with supplies, 3,700 cavalry horses and other draft animals, and 9 vessels including 3 gunboats. The Confederates lost 6,600 men, 700 horses, and 3 vessels, but they gained at least 600 supply wagons. Total numbers lost because of sickness are not known. The Red River Campaign had no positive effect on the outcome of the American Civil War. Because Union troops in Louisiana were not available to fight elsewhere, the campaign may have prolonged the War's slaughter by as much as two months.

PILGRIMS

Through 140 years, nearly everything had changed. Trees had overgrown farm fields. Areas that were wooded had been cleared. The muddy road where horses struggled and men fought and fled had been widened and paved for automobile traffic. A fence marked the boundary of Mansfield, Louisiana, State Commemorative Area, with granite monuments near the entrance. Across the highway was a sportsmen's club with a Confederate battle flag above the entrance. From its target range came the sound of gunfire.

Stephen and Pete had traveled five hours from New Orleans, on good Interstate highways, roughly following the Civil War route of their ancestor William Randall. The ride was pleasant and fast. It was a warm day under mostly blue skies. In March and April, 1864, William Randall's journey by steamboat up the Mississippi and Red Rivers to join his regiment took a week.

William Randall, a farmer from the hilly country south of Elmira, New York, had been 37 years old when he joined the Union Army in 1864. He left his wife at home with their four small children. He joined because the State of New York paid him a large bonus, and the army would give him more each month. William Randall was two years older than Stephen, who drove the car. Stephen was slender, like his ancestor, and a little taller. Pete had served in the military, but was not in combat. Stephen had been spared from being called to serve. Where William was poor, Stephen and Pete lived comfortably. Where he could read, write, and cipher, they were educated in universities. Where William struggled to provide for his family, they had the leisure to study history and to follow their interest in his experience, in a Civil War pilgrimage.

Stephen and Pete travelled on April 8, 2004, the 140th anniversary of the Battle of Mansfield, called the Battle of Sabine Cross Roads in Union Army reports. Private William H. Randall, Company K, 161st New York Volunteer Infantry Regiment, first saw combat in this battle, at the place called Pleasant Grove.

Inside the battlefield museum, site manager Don Smith was dressed as a Confederate soldier: eyeglasses with wire rims and small lenses, gingham shirt, heavy dark trousers and boots. His clothing was like his Confederate ancestors wore. He gave the visiting Yanks more help and kindness than was given to William Randall and his comrades. Mr Smith started a videotape that explained the battles on April 8 and 9, 1864. The video was professionally done, and the facts matched what Pete had learned through several years of research. Clearly, the Confederates won the Battle of Mansfield on April 8. It was a Union rout. On April 9 the armies fought again, the Battle of Pleasant Hill, which Union reports said was a Union victory because Confederate troops were driven back when they attacked the Union positions. But the videotape claimed it as a Confederate victory because the Union army had to withdraw after the battle ended. Opinions differ, and the video was made for the State of Louisiana, which had been one of the Confederate States of America.

Mr Smith told of a recent re-enactment by a group representing the Texas regiment in which one of his ancestors had served. They marched the three-mile route of the battle from the State Commemorative site to Pleasant Grove Farm, also called the Peach Orchard. He was unable to join the march, but he had hand-sewn a battle flag for his comrades.

Mr Smith provided copies of several pages of research notes about the actions and casualties of the 161st New York Volunteers, William Randall's regiment. After leaving the museum, Stephen and Pete walked the battlefield. Markers showed where Union regiments formed a line of battle, and were driven back. The 140-acre Mansfield state park covered only one-fifth of the area on which the first phase of the battle was fought. The soil was damp in wooded places. In cleared fields, anthills colonized dry earth. Where Union and Confederate soldiers bled into the ground, ants were now the victors.

Following the battle route, Stephen and Pete drove south on Louisiana highway 175. Roadside markers showed where Union soldiers formed their second and third lines of battle. The first line, at the Commemorative Area, collapsed under Confederate attack. Union troops were driven back into the column of supply wagons of their cavalry division. The second Union line was also driven back into their own supply wagons by the Confederate attack, and by fleeing soldiers, horses, and teamsters.

At the third line, the 161st New York Volunteers were posted at the front as skirmishers. There the hard-charging Confederates finally ran out of steam, and were stopped. The battle was reported as "a hard fight" in William Randall's diary. From his regiment, one man in seven was a casualty. Out of about 650 men in the 161st NYVI, 87 were killed, wounded, captured, or missing.

On the west side of highway 175, a rusting sign marked the third Union line of battle. On the east side, bulldozers and haul trucks had removed all trace of the peach orchard, Pleasant Grove Farm, the lane leading to the house, the contour of the land, and the battle. The battlefield was being strip-mined.

There should have been a feeling of outrage or sadness at that strip mine. Men fought and died there. But survivors fought again the next day, and continued the terrible War for another year. This place was not hallowed in memory like the Gettysburg, Antietam, and Shiloh battlefields. It was a place where fuel for an electric power plant could be dug from the ground. Commerce was grinding history to mud and dust.

Stephen and Pete followed the route of the armies a dozen miles south to the next battlefield. Union regiments had slipped away in the night and Confederates followed the next day, marching on a dirt road. The pilgrims rode in an air-conditioned car for twenty minutes on highway 175.

A modern map showed Pleasant Hill and Old Pleasant Hill, with no indication about where the battle was fought on April 9, 1864. A roadside marker and a memorial park said it was Old Pleasant Hill. Cows grazed in a nearby pasture. Grates in the road kept them from invading the little park.

Markers told of Dr. Eugene C. Poinboeuf, a local physician who died in 1994. He set up the park and was buried there with his wife Margie. He had no historic connection to the battle, other than living where it was fought. Dr. Poinboeuf had arranged for an 1864 *New York Tribune* report of the Battle of Pleasant Hill to be engraved on large stones. What might the reporter feel if he returned to find his words carved in stone?

Few people have heard of the Battles of Mansfield (or Sabine Cross Roads) and Pleasant Hill, except scholars of the American Civil War. The battles were fought in the Red River Campaign, a failed Union attempt to capture Shreveport. The campaign carried the destruction of war to western Louisiana, consuming lives and treasure. Strategically, it accomplished little.

NATCHITOCHES

Stephen and Pete spent that night near Natchitoches, Louisiana, where the Union Army camped before marching toward Mansfield. (Stephen's Cajun wife Nicole pronounced it "Nack'-a-tish.") They enjoyed a good dinner of seafood gumbo and

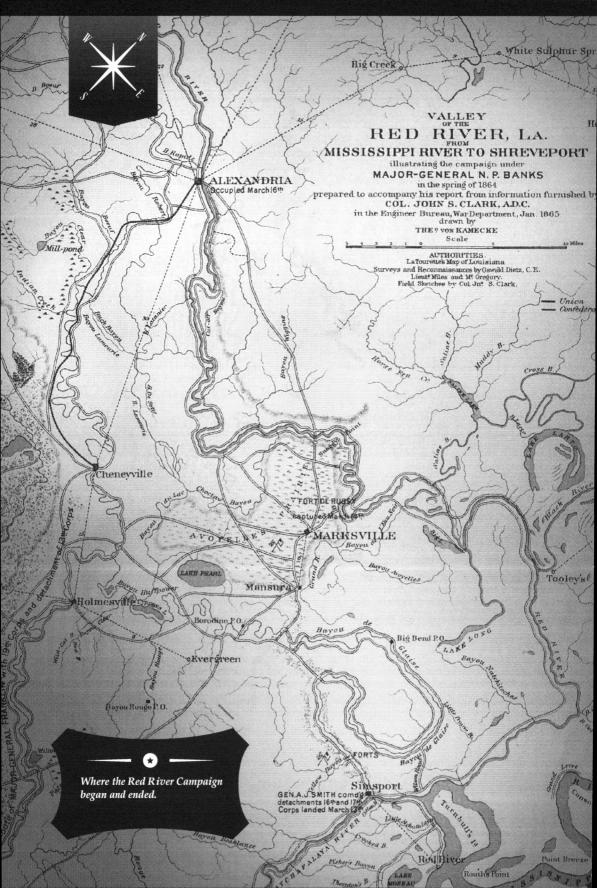

shrimp étouffée in a restaurant on the Cane River Lake waterfront. The town looked old, like many of its buildings had survived the Civil War.

The next day they explored the area. A few miles north, Grand Ecore had been the site of another Union encampment. Now the U.S. Army Corps of Engineers had a Waterways Visitor Center there. Displays explained how the Corps of Engineers kept the Red River open for boat and barge traffic. Before construction of the modern system of levees and dams, the courses of Louisiana rivers (the Mississippi, Red, Atchafalaya, and Cane) changed each year in spring floods. Cane River became a lake when its connections to the Red River silted shut.

In his book about the 161st New York Regiment, Private John Merwin wrote of a convent on a high bluff overlooking Natchitoches. The volunteer in the tourist center did not know of a convent, but she provided copies of several articles about local history. Natchitoches was the seat of a Roman Catholic bishop. One article mentioned a school for girls on the hill where a "normal school" had trained teachers. In 2004, modern buildings of Northwest Louisiana State University stood there.

The day was Good Friday, a holiday in Louisiana. Faithful Catholic families from St. Denis church were on a different kind of pilgrimage than Stephen and Pete. They followed their priest through the town, stopping to pray the stations of the cross. A police officer held traffic for them on the main street along Cane River Lake.

A map from the Natchitoches tourist center showed a route south along Cane River Lake past seven plantations. Pete knew this was the route on which the Union Army retreated in 1864. Many pre-war buildings were looted and burned by retreating soldiers. What was there in 2004 did not look like what William Randall saw.

When slaves did the work, plantations raised sugar cane or cotton. Stephen and Pete saw homes surrounded by tall pecan trees aligned in neat rows. Under the trees, bright yellow flowers bloomed in pastures where cattle grazed. A plantation called Little Eva was named as the home of slave driver Simon Legree in the Harriet Beecher Stowe novel **Uncle Tom's Cabin**.

The road crossed Cane River at Monett's Ferry. A nearly hidden marker named the crossing, and a rusty historic marker on the other side mentioned the battle. In a roadside field, stubble and bits of cotton littered the ground. Wildflowers added pink to the green river bank. Between river and field was a dirt track, which might have looked like it did when soldiers fought there on April 23, 1864.

The highway took Stephen and Pete to Alexandria, where the Red River was hidden behind a high levee. A medical center stood where Union soldiers sweat and struggled to build temporary dams that allowed Admiral David Porter's fleet of gunboats to pass the Red River falls. In the 20th century, the U.S. Army Corps of Engineers blasted the falls and rapids to make way for concrete locks and dams. There was no sign of the Civil War. Union soldiers had burned Alexandria as they retreated.

The pilgrims followed the Union Army retreat along Louisiana route 1 and the Red River levee to Marksville, site of another battle that William Randall mentioned in his diary. A side road took them through Mansura, where a marker reported a battle, and another side road took them through Moreauville. Bayou de Glaize was the last battle in the Red River Campaign. At Simmesport they crossed the Atchafalaya River on a high bridge. In May 1864, Colonel Joseph Bailey anchored steamboats side by side, and laid planks between them to form a bridge that the Union Army crossed with their horse-drawn wagons and guns.

The highway crossed Morganza Spillway. Morganza Bend in the Mississippi River was the site of a large Union Army camp. Many soldiers died there from chronic diarrhea, which was caused by polluted drinking water. After the War ended, ex-slaves were hired to dig up the bodies, which were reburied in National Cemeteries at Vicksburg and Baton Rouge.

Except on bridges, of which there were few, the Louisiana rivers were completely hidden behind modern levees. Across the Mississippi River was Port Hudson, where the 161st New York Regiment fought in spring 1863, before William Randall enlisted. Steamboats carried Union troops on the rivers. The modern map showed a ferry crossing nearby.

On the opposite shore of the Mississippi River, Stephen and Pete drove through the old town of St. Francisville, then southeast to Port Hudson. A State Commemorative Area preserved much of the original Confederate fortification there. Port Hudson was very strong. It was besieged and attacked by Union troops for several months, but they failed to capture it. After the heavily fortified city of Vicksburg surrendered on July 4, 1863, to Union General Ulysses S. Grant, the Confederate commander at Port Hudson also surrendered.

In Port Hudson National Cemetery, Union soldiers who died in the siege and attacks were buried. It was outside the battlefield area and down a side road, nearly surrounded by a chemical plant. Here, industry deferred to the cemetery.

SUMMER IN THE DEEP SOUTH

MARCH 23-JUNE 16, 1864

Private William Randall had survived the battles, skirmishes, long marches, hard labor, and illness of the Red River Campaign. The 161st New York Volunteer Infantry Regiment was in camp at Morganza Bend, Louisiana, about fifty miles up the Mississippi River from Baton Rouge. William slipped into the routine of summer life in Union Army camps along the river.

The daily schedule in camp was like this:

Reveille, first call	5:50 a.m.	Company Drill	10:00 to 11:30
Reveille, second call	6:00	Recall from fatigue duty	11:55 a.m.
Roll Call immediately after Reveille		Dinner Call	12:00 Noon
Clean up quarters	6:15	Battalion Drill	2:30 to 4:30 p.m.
Breakfast Call	6:30	Recall from fatigue duty	4:35
Surgeons Call	7:00	Dress Parade	4:45
Squad Drill	7:30 to 8:30	Tattoo	8:00
Post the guard	9:00	Taps	8:15 p.m.

In a letter written February 13, 1863, from New Orleans, Sergeant Lewis E. Fitch described the daily routine to his parents:

 *We rise every morning at six and get our breakfast ready to eat immediately after roll call at half past six, at half past seven we have squad drill, each of the Sergeants taking a squad of men under his charge and putting them through a course of sprints. I have just been drilling a squad until half past eight; then we are at leisure until ten when we fall in for drill until half past eleven; then we get dinner, and rest until half past two, when the grand Brigade drill comes on lasting until five, supper is then to be got and then nothing more is done until roll call at eight when we are tired enough to go to bed...The drum is beating for a drill and I must stop until after dinner.*

In the summer, days and nights were oppressively hot and damp, but there was no change to adapt the daily routine to the climate. William's day book records mail from and to his family, drills and inspections, and frequent funerals for comrades who were dying of dysentery or chronic diarrhea. The connection between disease, drinking water, and seepage from latrines was suspected but not clearly understood.

MONDAY 23 *We lay in camp on the Mississippi River bank. Called out on company inspection. Wrote home.*

TUESDAY, MAY 24, 1864 *Laid in camp all day. A fine shower just at night. Thomas Watson and Drias Soper got here the 22nd.*

"Drias" was Private Darius A. Soper, age 21, who enlisted on February 15, 1864. Private Thomas J. Watson, age 21, enlisted on February 8, 1864.

WEDNESDAY 25 *Wrote home. Laid in camp all day long. Very fine weather now. Lieutenant Davis came back to the regiment.*

Parvis Davis, age 36, enrolled at Elmira and mustered in on December 28, 1863. He was First Lieutenant of Company F. He commanded the group of 77 men who travelled with William from New York to Louisiana in the spring of 1864.

THURSDAY 26 *Lay in camp today. Called out on inspection. Patch up my pockets.*

FRIDAY, MAY 27, 1864 *Laid in camp till 10 o'clock AM then I was called out on picket, and wrote a letter home and put it in the office.*

SATURDAY 28 *We are on picket till 10 o'clock AM and come in camp. It is a very fine day. A cannon was shot three times over a dead boes [?].*

SUNDAY 29 *Laid in camp all day. Only making shade over our tents. Wrote part of a letter home. Went to meeting tonight.*

MONDAY, MAY 30, 1864 *Finished the letter home and sent it, went to meeting at night. One brigade went out skirmishing. Captured some horses and some rebels.*

TUESDAY 31 *Laid in camp all day long. Drew flour for the first time. Went to meeting at night. Fine day.*

A commissary sergeant issued daily rations to the troops. The official U.S. Army daily ration allowed each man one 16-oz. biscuit (hardtack, pilot bread, or crackers) or 22 oz. of bread or flour, 1-1/4 lb. of fresh or salt meat or 3/4 lb. of bacon. In June 1864 the ration was increased by 6 oz. of flour or 4 oz. of hard bread and 3 lb. of potatoes. For each 100 men, there was an additional daily allowance of 8 gal. beans, 10 lb. rice or hominy, 10 lb. coffee, 15 lb. sugar, 4 gal. vinegar, and 2 lb. salt. Having flour meant that the soldiers could make fresh bread instead of eating hardtack.

WEDNESDAY, JUNE 1 *The general inspection. Laid in camp all day.*

THURSDAY, JUNE 2, 1864 *Had a mail letter from home. Wrote a letter home and one to father-in-law. Sent them both. Laid in camp.*

FRIDAY 3 *Went out on picket. Rained all night long very hard. Company drill in the morning.*

SATURDAY 4 *Stayed out on picket till eleven o'clock AM. Come in camp. Fix tent. Rained a hard shower at night. Funeral Deloss Ayers.*

Private Delos Ayres, age 19, enlisted on February 23, 1864. He died of chronic diarrhea.

SUNDAY, JUNE 5, 1864 *Fix for inspection. Went to funeral Gore A. Whitney. Inspection at five o'clock PM. Meeting at night.*

Private George A. Whiteney enlisted on September 9, 1862, at Elmira and mustered into Company B. He was 21 years old when he died of chronic diarrhea.

MONDAY 6 *Went out foraging, the regiment 17 miles and our company went one mile. Then we rode out and back five miles, then we march into camp.*

TUESDAY 7 *Laid in camp all day. The company drank closes. [?] I felt very bad. Dreamed about home.*

WEDNESDAY, JUNE 8, 1864 *Laid in camp today. Got an order [for] one dollar on the sutler. Got a can for condensed milk. Drill at night.*

A sutler was a civilian merchant who sold goods in camp. Newspapers, books, food, tobacco, and razors were on the approved list. Alcohol could be sold to officers but not to enlisted men. Sometimes a sutler sold it to them anyway. The regimental order book reports that a Council of Administration of three officers was appointed on May 4, 1864, to inspect the records of the sutler, to set the tariff for his goods, and to inspect his weights and measures.

> **THURSDAY 9** *We are ordered out to march over the levee. Camp on the green. Put up our tents, dug latrine and so forth.*

> **FRIDAY 10** *Got a mail from home, three letters, [and] one in James Decker letter. Went out on drill. Wrote home a letter.*

There were two men named James B. Decker in the regiment, both Privates. "James the elder," age 24, enlisted in Company C on January 14, 1864. "James the younger," age 18, enlisted in Company D on February 9, 1864. Someone at home was saving a few cents postage by sending letters for two soldiers together.

> **SATURDAY, JUNE 11, 1864** *Went out on picket. 19 Army Corps on review. Rain all through the review. Charles M. Swain died at night.*

The review in the rain was for Brigadier General William H. Emory, who had commanded XIX Corps since May 2. General Emory led First Division, XIX Corps, at Pleasant Grove in the Battle of Sabine Cross Roads.

Private Charles M. Swain, Company K, age 22, enlisted on January 14, 1864. He died of chronic diarrhea. In his book **Battle Cry of Freedom**, historian James McPherson wrote, "Three diseases were the principal killers of the War: diarrhea/dysentery, typhoid, and pneumonia. In the south they faced other deadly diseases, malaria and yellow fever." In the 161st New York Regiment, more men died of chronic diarrhea than of Confederate bullets.

> **SUNDAY 12** *Come in from picket, went to funeral. Don't feel very well. Got a letter from home. It rains now.*

> **MONDAY 13** *Laid in camp today. Brigade drill at five o'clock PM.*

> **TUESDAY, JUNE 14, 1864** *I am excused today. 19 Corps out on a review. Today fine weather. Wrote home.*

This review was to honor Major General Daniel E. Sickles, who lost a leg while commanding III Corps at the Battle of Gettysburg. Sickles was a New York politician who killed his wife's lover in 1859, then became the first man acquitted of murder because of insanity.

> **WEDNESDAY 15** *Laid in camp all day. The Colonel [has] gone up to Vicksburg to report. It rains now.*

> **THURSDAY 16** *Laid in camp. Called out on regiment drill. Funeral John Lusis.*

The dead were buried as quickly as possible, near where they died in camps and battlefields. Temporary grave markers faded and fell in the wind and rain. Damp soil caused bodies and clothing to decay, and metal insignia to corrode, so that later identification was usually impossible. After the War ended, the U.S. Army Quartermaster Department hired ex-slaves to dig up all the graves of Union soldiers that could be found, and moved the remains to new National Cemeteries. Many graves were never found.

Private John Lewis, age 36, enlisted on December 25, 1863, and died in the regimental hospital at Morganza Bend, Louisiana. He is buried in the National Cemetery at Port Hudson, Louisiana. Delos Ayres, George Whiteney, and Charles M. Swain may also be there. Cemetery records were published in several volumes called *The Roll of Honor: Names of Soldiers Who Died in Defence of the American Union*. Remains from Morganza Bend were moved to Port Hudson, where Private Lewis was placed in one of only 500 graves whose occupants were identified. About 2,500 graves at Port Hudson are marked "Unknown."

A JOURNEY TO VICKSBURG
(June 17–July 22)

Vicksburg, Mississippi, had been in Union hands since July 4, 1863, when it was captured after a siege of nearly two months by a Union army under Major General Ulysses S. Grant. It was an important transportation point where goods arriving by railroad were shipped on or across the Mississippi River.

In June 1864, the 161st New York Volunteer Infantry Regiment was ordered to Vicksburg. Their commanding officer, Lieutenant Colonel William B. Kinsey, had gone ahead. The Regiment was to join a new Engineer Brigade under Colonel Joseph Bailey, who had distinguished himself by constructing the dam at Alexandria, Louisiana, which saved Admiral Porter's fleet of gunboats. Now, Colonel Bailey had a new assignment.

Major General Edward R. S. Canby, commanding general of the Union Military Division of West Mississippi, was planning a new campaign. He wanted to move against Shreveport along the line of a partially built railroad that ran west from Vicksburg. In support of the campaign, Colonel Bailey was to complete the railroad.

For William Randall and the other soldiers of the 161st NYVI Regiment, daily routine and the weather at Vicksburg were like Morganza Bend, but the scenery was a little different.

> **FRIDAY, JUNE 17, 1864** *Got a mail from Rufus B. Gleason. Went out on picket. Orders came to be ready to move with three days rations.*

Having control of the Mississippi River allowed the Union army to move its troops where they were needed. Military transports and commercial steamboats, towboats, and barges travelled freely on the river, and all were used to haul troops, animals, and supplies.

> **SATURDAY 18** *Was relieved at 10 o'clock PM. Went onto the boat at 8 o'clock AM. Started out 9 o'clock AM up the river. Stop at Natchez one hour.*
>
> **SUNDAY 19** *Then had a meeting. Started out up the river. Run all night [and] all day till sundown. Landed at Vicksburg in Mississippi country.*
>
> **MONDAY, JUNE 20, 1864** *Laid on the steamboat all night. March off from the boat 5 AM. Up through the city and camp 1 mile from the depot. Drew bread.*
>
> **TUESDAY 21** *Laid in camp all day. Wrote home. Very hard rain.*
>
> **WEDNESDAY 22** *Laid in camp all day. A very hard rain.*
>
> **THURSDAY, JUNE 23, 1864** *Laid in camp all day long. There are eight or ten sick men taken to the general hospital down town.*
>
> **FRIDAY 24** *There was a colored man shot for shooting his wife. Two colored regiments marched up in a line and 12 of them shot him on his coffin. Lay in camp.*

Private Cornelius Thompson, Company A, 48th U.S. Colored Infantry Regiment, was a 35-year-old farmer from Mississippi and an ex-slave. He was convicted by a general court martial on June 16 of the premeditated murder of a civilian laundress, Miss Martha Richardson, in his regiment's camp at Vicksburg.

Former slaves were first enlisted into the Union Army's Corps D'Afrique as laborers. Later they were armed, and their units were designated U.S. Colored Infantry Regiments. They served under white officers, many of whom were promoted from other Union regiments. A Corporal or Sergeant might find a commission as Lieutenant or Captain in a U.S. Colored Regiment, while a Lieutenant might gain the rank of Major. Higher rank earned more pay, of course.

In a March 5, 1863, letter to his sister, Corporal Samuel A. Johnson of the 161st Regiment wrote,

There was a Negro Regiment here called 4th La. Native Guard. When they first came here they had a number of black officers but the officers from other regiments made such a fuss about them that they were all discharged which left fifteen vacancies in the Regiment. That was some four weeks ago. I was just about the same as offered a Captain's commission but did not pay any attention to it until yesterday. I happened to pass their headquarters so I went in to see the Colonel but was just one day too late. All the vacancies were filled.

The newspaper *Steuben Farmers Advocate* in Bath, New York, published this on August 12, 1863:

> One of the boys writing from Baton Rouge says that Lieutenant Powers, of Avoca, has accepted a commission as Captain for the purpose of recruiting a company of negro volunteers. Volunteering by the blacks is a 'big thing.' The writer says that a squad of men go out, seize the negroes, taking them from the plantations, bring them into camp telling them they will now be made soldiers. As soon as the darkies are told this story they are suddenly afflicted with diverse diseases. But it's no use to murmur, Lincoln's soldiers free the negro and he must fight for his new Massa.

African-American soldiers were led by white officers until after World War II, when President Harry S. Truman ordered an end to segregation in the U.S. Armed Services. In the third and fourth generations of Americans born after the Civil War ended slavery, African-Americans were finally allowed to earn positions as commanding generals and admirals, as Chairman of the Joint Chiefs of Staff, and as civilian secretaries of the U.S. Armed Services.

SATURDAY 25 *I went down town and saw the city in AM. PM went around about the camp ground. Rest of the time laid in camp.*

SUNDAY, JUNE 26, 1864 *I am on camp guard. Went on at eight o'clock AM. Stayed on till eight o'clock the next morning AM.*

MONDAY 27 *Come off guard this morning. Got two letters from home, one from Mother. Wrote a letter home.*

"Mother" was William's wife Cynthia. His own mother is thought to have died between 1855 and 1860.

TUESDAY 28 *Went on police duty. The rest of the time laid in camp all day.*

WEDNESDAY, JUNE 29, 1864 *Went down town. Got some ripe peaches and some ripe apples and saw the saw mills, then picked some greens.*

THURSDAY 30 *Laid in camp all day. Drew flour. Very warm weather.*

Lieutenant General Ulysses S. Grant, General in Chief of the United States Army, ordered that plans for the Shreveport Campaign were to be set aside for the time being. Grant saw clearly how the War had to be won: Attack and hold General Robert E. Lee's Confederate Army in Virginia, destroy their food sources in the Shenandoah Valley, and divide the Confederacy east of the Mississippi River by capturing Atlanta and destroying rail transportation routes. Two divisions of the Union XIX Corps were transferred east, where they fought in the Shenandoah Valley Campaign. Other forces from west of the Mississippi River would soon be sent to attack Mobile Bay, Alabama, to hold Confederate forces who might otherwise defend Atlanta. Campaigns west of the Mississippi could wait until the Confederates were defeated in the east.

Near the end of June, Colonel Bailey learned that the Shreveport Campaign and construction of the Vicksburg and Shreveport Railroad were postponed. Work shifted to repairing the railroad between Vicksburg and Jackson, Mississippi. While generals planned strategy, the 161st New York Regiment continued to labor, drill, and endure summer at Vicksburg.

FRIDAY, JULY 1 *Got a letter from home and wrote one back home. Laid in camp all day. Had a very hard rain.*

SATURDAY, JULY 2, 1864 *Wrote to Electa and Mother. Laid in camp all day. Went out to pray under a shade tree. Had a good time.*

Electa Randall Shaw was William's younger sister.

SUNDAY 3 *Laid in camp all day. Felt very bad headache, the P__[?]tare in my head. Had an apple shortcake made by a wench.*

MONDAY 4 *I don't feel very well. The cannonading commenced at four o'clock AM. Kept up till six o'clock PM. Had 12 mules for each wagon. A long train of wagons loaded with _[?]nses[?].*

In a letter to his sister dated July 9, Private Sylvester L. Retan wrote,

It was the dullest Fourth that I ever saw. There was a salute fired at sunrise and at sundown. There was another salute fired of a hundred and thirty guns. It was a very warm day. I stayed to camp all day, but at night I went down town. There was splendid fireworks . . . one Roman candle and skyrockets, and a whirlygig. You can image [sic] they were splendid.

TUESDAY JULY 5, 1864 *Wrote to Rufus B. Gleason. Stayed around camp all day. Drew one rubber [blanket], one drawers, one socks, one tent piece.*

Rufus B. Gleason was the brother of William Randall's wife Cynthia.

WEDNESDAY 6 *Went out on fatigue [duty]. Went down to the mills. Piled up lumber AM, PM loaded wagon and was sick.*

THURSDAY 7 *Excused from duty. Barber orderly sergeant died. Another one to the hospital died. Had two meetings, one the chaplain [was] there, other up under an oak tree. John went to pray.*

Charles E. Barbour, age 25, enlisted on February 19, 1864. He was promoted to sergeant in June. He died at City Hospital, Vicksburg. The Roll of Honor reports that he was buried in Mississippi River National Cemetery at Vicksburg.

The chaplain was Reverend William E. Jones, a Presbyterian minister from Bath, New York. He joined the regiment on April 23, 1863, at Baton Rouge. After the War he wrote a history of the 161st New York Volunteers, which he published at Bath in October, 1865.

The other soldier who died was Private John Huntington, age 21, Company I, who enlisted at Jasper on February 19, 1864. He died of "congestion" on July 4.

"John" who "went to pray" may have been John McLean, First Sergeant of Company K. Other men named John in Company K at this time were Privates John Brown, John Lloyd, and John Wheaton. All survived the War and were mustered out after it ended.

FRIDAY, JULY 8, 1864 *Excused from duty. A man died, his name was Chafa. It is very warm. Had a good prayer meeting at ten o'clock PM.*

Private Ezra Chaffee, age 41, enlisted on December 29, 1863. He died "at company quarters." He was in Company I.

SATURDAY 9 *Excused from duty. Had a fine prayer meeting. Got a mail, one letter from home. Very hot weather.*

SUNDAY 10 *Excused from duty. Had two prayer meetings in camp. Some went down town to meeting.*

MONDAY, JULY 11, 1864 *Excused from duty. Wrote a letter home. Hard rain storm. Very hot sun.*

TUESDAY 12 *Excused from duty. Cook a mess of greens. Had a hard rain. Hot sunshine.*

WEDNESDAY 13 *Went on guard. My head ached very hard all day. Had a cucumber and a bowl of sour milk.*

THURSDAY, JULY 14, 1864 *Wrote letter home. Laid in camp all day long. Very warm and hot. A new doctor came, the old doctor left.*

Regimental Surgeon Louis Darling, age 60, was discharged for disability on April 13, 1864. Philo K. Stoddard served as Assistant Surgeon from September 1863, until September 1865. William D. Murray, who had been Assistant Surgeon in the 100th New York Regiment, was mustered into the 161st as the new Surgeon on July 16, 1864.

FRIDAY 15 *Feel some better today. Laid in camp all day. Patch my trousers. Very hot sun.*

SATURDAY 16 *Ordered out on a dress parade. Laid in camp all day. Very hot sun.*

SUNDAY, JULY 17, 1864 *Out on drill. Regiment out on dress parade. Had a fine meeting. It is a very hot day.*

MONDAY 18 *Out on company drill. Out on company dress parade. Had a hard head ache. Very hot sun.*

TUESDAY 19 *I was called out to guard wagon train. [I was] sent for to sign pay rolls. Got fifty-five dollars in money.*

As a private, William earned $13 a month. On June 20, 1864, the pay for privates was increased to $16. William also received a bounty payment of $20 per month. Charges for clothing and for purchases from the sutler were deducted from his pay. Inflation in 1864 and 1865 reduced the value of William's pay, so that $55 in 1864 was equivalent to only about $746 in 2010. He sent most of his pay home to his wife.

WEDNESDAY, JULY 20, 1864 *Come in off guard and sent forty dollars by express to Elmira to Cynthia Jane Randall.*

THURSDAY 21 *Went to Jermire Reed funeral about four miles. Tired out and rode part of the way back. Bought some fish.*

Private Jeremiah Reed enlisted on August 22, 1862 at New Berlin, Chenango County, and mustered into Company K. He was promoted to Corporal on June 1, 1864. He died of chronic diarrhea, age 28 years.

FRIDAY 22 *We were ordered to get in readiness to march at any time in thirty minutes. Laid in camp all day in readiness.*

TO ARKANSAS AND BACK
(July 23–August 19)

The White River in Arkansas was the line of communication for a Union Army commanded by Major General Frederick Steele. When Confederate forces threatened traffic on the river, Union troops under Brigadier General George H. Gordon were sent to protect shipping. The Engineer Brigade under Colonel Joseph Bailey was part of General Gordon's force.

> **SATURDAY, JULY 23, 1864** *I went on camp guard then the order came to march down to the boat. We march down to the landing, laid two hours, went on board, started out in the afternoon.*
>
> **SUNDAY 24** *Went all night, all day Sunday, and all night. Stopped and put on cables twice.*

"Cables" were heavy ropes, not telegraph messages. They tied a vessel securely to a dock or the shore.

> **MONDAY 25** *We started out and ran up the river to the mouth of White River and stopped there for further orders.*

The 161st New York Volunteer Infantry Regiment was mostly embarked in the transport *Universe*, with a few men in the *Clara Bell*, which also carried part of 6th Michigan Regiment. The boats became separated and a Confederate battery fired at the *Clara Bell*. She was forced ashore and landed her troops, then another shell set her on fire. The soldiers were picked up by another boat. William does not mention the incident so he must have travelled in the *Universe*.

Private Charles M. Couch of Company C wrote a letter to his mother about this trip. On July 28, from White River Landing, he wrote,

> *We left Vicksburg last Saturday and we got here on Monday morning and have been here ever since. One of the boats that came up the River with us was fired into and burned up. There were four companies of the 6th Michigan [Regiment] on board but there were only two of them killed and wounded. One of our men was on board of her and he was wounded. There was one man in our company that fell overboard, we suppose, and was lost. We have not heard anything from him, any way. His name was Johnson.*

Private Couch's mother never saw him again. He died of chronic diarrhea on August 24, 1864, at University Hospital in New Orleans. He had enlisted on December 29, 1863, age 21 years.

The man who was lost and presumed drowned was Private George W. Johnson, age 27, who enlisted at Elmira on September 17, 1862. There was another Private George W. Johnson of about the same age in Company E. He enlisted at Catharine, Schuyler County, on October 25, 1862, and mustered out at Elmira on September 20, 1865.

Chaplain William E. Jones also wrote about the expedition to Arkansas.

> The weather was intensely hot; the water, a mean mixture of the Mississippi and White Rivers, and the atmosphere very insalubrious and exceedingly depressing. White River Landing — which can only boast of one small store and a few negro huts — is on Island Number 73, formed by the Mississippi, Arkansas and White Rivers. Nothing of interest occurred here except the frequent arrival of transports, with troops from Memphis and other places bound for St. Charles and Devall's Bluff on the White River.

> **TUESDAY, JULY 26, 1864** *Was on guard on the boats. Laid in camp on the bank of the Mississippi at the mouth of White River. Ordered on the boat at 10 o'clock at night.*

> **WEDNESDAY 27** *Laid on the boat till this morning. At 1 o'clock PM then we were ordered back to camp then detail after detail all day long.*

> **THURSDAY 28** *We laid in camp all day. Bought a big fish. Got a bottle.*

William's "bottle" probably contained liquor, which was generally forbidden to enlisted men. In a letter to his sister dated March 5, 1863, Corporal Samuel A. Johnson wrote, "You asked me if he [a friend named George] could get liquor. No one but commissioned officers can get it and they have to have a permit from the Provost Marshall. You cannot even get a glass of cider. Nothing but spruce beer and that is as weak as dishwater." In spite of the rule, sutlers sometimes sold liquor to soldiers. Since it was forbidden, the price was increased. William was probably hung over the next day.

> **FRIDAY, JULY 29, 1864** *I was called out on fatigue cleaning up the camp. I was very badly chafed [?].*

> **SATURDAY 30** *Laid in camp all day. Just at night wrote a letter home. Very warm and hot sun. Rain at night.*

> **SUNDAY 31** *Was detailed to fatigue duty carrying wood on the boat. Laid in camp all day long.*

> **MONDAY, AUGUST 1, 1864** *Laid in camp all day. We were ordered to get ready to move at twenty minutes notice.*

Soldiers used free time in camp to write letters, read newspapers and letters from home, clean and repair clothing and equipment, clean rifles and bayonets, polish brass buttons and insignia, etc. Inspections were frequent, with the troops in line and an officer or sergeant checking that every man was up to standard. Rust on a rifle barrel or dirt on a uniform would be punished with extra duty.

TUESDAY 2 *I was called out on picket. Stood one trick. Was released for brigade inspections.*

WEDNESDAY 3 *Laid in camp all day long. Wrote Rufus Gleason a letter and sent it.*

THURSDAY, AUGUST 4, 1864 *This brigade was ordered to get ready to move in a half hour notice, then laid in camp all day long.*

After ten days in Arkansas at the mouth of White River, 161st New York Regiment returned to Morganza Bend, Louisiana. A few days later they were ordered to join an attack on Mobile Bay, Alabama. The attack on Mobile was intended to divert Confederate troops from the defense of Atlanta.

FRIDAY 5 *Our regiment and Sixth Michigan Regiment were ordered to march on the boats then started down the river. Three boat loads.*

SATURDAY 6 *They ran all night and all day but two hours stop to put on wood. Got melon. Then got to Vicksburg at dark.*

SUNDAY, AUGUST 7, 1864 *Ran across the river, put on coal, ran back in the morning. Laid till 10 o'clock AM. Started out for Morganza Bend. Ran the rest of the day and night. Letter from home.*

MONDAY 8 *Stopped at Natchez four hours then ran till 11 o'clock AM. Went in camp at Morganza Bend then on fatigue the rest of the day.*

TUESDAY 9 *Went on camp fatigue. Laid in camp the rest of the day. Good news from Mobile: 800 prisoners and 28 guns.*

WEDNESDAY, AUGUST 10, 1864 *We laid in camp all day. Wrote a letter home and wrote a letter to Electa A. Shaw.*

THURSDAY 11 *Was out on drill. I got a letter from home and wrote one home. Stayed in camp all day. Five boat loads of soldiers landed opposite our camp.*

FRIDAY 12 *Laid there all day partly unloaded. Then they struck tents. 150[th New York Regiment], 6th Michigan [Regiment] started for home. We laid in camp all [day].*

SATURDAY, AUGUST 13, 1864 *Our regiment ordered to get in readiness to go aboard the boat in an hour. Then the order is countermanded. Brigade tonls[?] took aboard.*

SUNDAY 14 *Went on fatigue. There are rumors of all kinds through camp about moving. Stayed in camp the rest of the day.*

MONDAY 15 *Ordered to go aboard the boat. Started down the Mississippi River. Got here to New Orleans at 9 o'clock PM. Stayed aboard all night.*

TUESDAY, AUGUST 16, 1864 *Laid here at the dock waiting for fuel [and] orders. Started 7 o'clock PM. Ran all night.*

WEDNESDAY 17 *Stopped at Baton Rouge, then ran up to Fort Hudson, then up to Morganza and went in camp to company on fatigue.*

THURSDAY 18 *Laid in camp. Orders came that this regiment [is] in the 17 Corps AM, PM in 19 Corps and so forth.*

FRIDAY, AUGUST 19, 1864 *Ordered out on company inspection. I laid in camp the rest of the day. Orders came to move at half past seven o'clock.*

MOBILE BAY
(August 20–September 8)

Mobile Bay was a strategic point, an excellent harbor on the Gulf of Mexico. The Alabama and Tombigbee Rivers and two rail lines gave it good access to inland Alabama. The harbor was heavily fortified and mined by Confederate forces and was guarded in the summer of 1864 by three wooden gunboats and an ironclad. Additional ironclads were under construction to break the Union blockade.

Forts Gaines, Morgan, and Powell guarded the entrances to Mobile Bay. A Union campaign against them began on August 3, 1864. The Union Navy entered Mobile Bay on August 5 and captured the Confederate ironclad Tennessee. This was the naval battle in which Admiral David Farragut said, "Damn the torpedoes! Full speed ahead!" Civil War "torpedoes" are now called contact mines.

Fort Gaines on Dauphin Island was attacked by Union troops of the XIII Corps under Major General Gordon Granger and was shelled by Admiral Farragut's ships. The Confederates there surrendered on August 8. Then Union forces moved across the main ship channel to Fort Morgan. Siege guns were sent from New Orleans, and additional troops were ordered to Mobile Bay, including the 161st New York Volunteer Infantry Regiment.

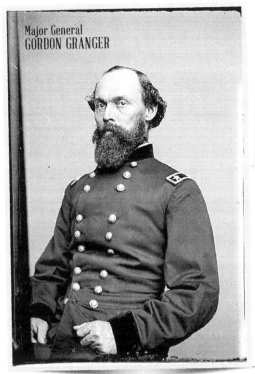

Major General GORDON GRANGER

FORT MORGAN-Before

FORT MORGAN After

SATURDAY 20 *It rained till 10 o'clock AM. Laid in camp the rest of the day. Orders just came to move to New Orleans. Went on board the boat.*

SUNDAY 21 *Started out. Stopped at Fort Hudson at 12 o'clock, then to Baton Rouge, then to New Orleans at 6 o'clock PM. Went aboard a ship named Hoby.*

Regiments from XIX Corps that were transferred to the east took their sick and wounded members. When 161st New York Regiment left the unhealthful camp at Morganza Bend, they also took their sick comrades with them. Some men were too ill to travel beyond New Orleans and were taken to St James Hospital. This was the "St James Infirmary" that gave its name to a famous blues song.

The ship in which the 161st Regiment sailed from New Orleans was *Cahawba* (William's "Hoby"). Channel pilots were needed to navigate through shifting channels at the mouth of the Mississippi River and at the entrance to Mobile Bay. Before William and his regiment arrived at Mobile Bay, the Confederates surrendered Fort Morgan.

MONDAY, AUGUST 22, 1864 *Started out at 3 o'clock PM. Stopped at Fort Jackson, then stopped at Fort Philip, then ran down near the mouth of the river, got a pilot, ran out.*

TUESDAY 23 *In the Gulf then up the ocean to the mouth of Mobile Bay. Got a pilot to run us in. Fort Morgan surrendered this morning at 4 o'clock AM.*

WEDNESDAY 24 *We got into the fort at 9 o'clock AM. Laid there till 6 o'clock PM then got on another boat. Ran up 3 miles. Laid on the dock. Went in camp.*

THURSDAY, AUGUST 25, 1864 *We were ordered to get ready to go aboard at 7 o'clock AM. Stayed till 2 o'clock PM. Went on board. Started out across the bay to Seward Point [and] landed.*

FRIDAY 26 *March of a mile then back and camp this morning. Went on fatigue [duty] repairing the wharf out into the bay some seventy-five or eighty rods.*

In his history of the regiment, Chaplain William E. Jones wrote about the night of August 25-26 and the following days:

> We spread our blankets for the night on the narrow shell road that runs for miles through low, marshy ground. And such a night of trouble! Fires were built every few yards as a protection against mosquitoes, but all in vain. They filled the air about us and "presented their bills" with such frequency, importunity, and success, that it proved a night of torture. Scarcely any of us succeeded in obtaining more than a few minutes' sleep. To this annoyance followed that of brackish water, which made our tea and coffee almost unbearable. Then, worse than all, our provisions began to fail, and for a few days some of us were in great straits for something to eat. To this day, the Point is remembered in the Regiment under the expressive and appropriate soubriquet of "Point Misery."

Private Cornelius Osterhout of Company A also complained about bad water and mosquitoes. In a letter to his mother dated September 8, 1864, he wrote, "We have been to Mobile and took three forts. They had about 200 cannons mounted on them. We took one gun and a gunboat and sank one. We did not like it there. We could not get any fresh water. It was all salt." He added, "The weather is warm and the mosquitoes have been near eating us up when we were at Mobile."

Complaints about insects were not new. Fifteen months earlier, as 161st New York Volunteer Infantry Regiment began their first summer in the south, a paragraph about the pesky bugs appeared in a Bath, New York, newspaper, the *Steuben Farmers Advocate*. On May 27, 1863, the editor published a letter written May 2nd, from Lieutenant J. F. Little at Baton Rouge, to A. L. Underhill:

The only thing now to be feared in this Department are the mosquitoes, which are terrible. When we go on picket we either have to take our mosquito bars along or place our backs against a tree to prevent any attack from the rear, and stand with a sword in one hand and a revolver in the other to keep at bay the swarms of midge, mosquitoes, Gallinippers and every other imaginable thing that can add to one's torment. In addition to all this, the ground is covered with things creeping innumerable.

While others complained of mosquitoes and bad water, William Randall wrote of eating oysters. In Elmira, oysters were a delicacy.

> **SATURDAY 27** *Laid in camp all day. Only got some oysters, then moved up to the fort and camp.*
>
> **SUNDAY, AUGUST 28, 1864** *Laid in camp all day long. Wrote a letter home. Orders read to not go in the water. Hard rain.*
>
> **MONDAY 29** *Laid in camp all day long. No further orders. Oysters aplenty.*
>
> **TUESDAY 30** *Laid in camp all day long. Nothing of great importance. Only got a few oysters.*
>
> **WEDNESDAY, AUGUST 31, 1864** *Regiment was mustered at 6 o'clock AM. Went on fatigue making breastworks two hours AM. Laid in camp all day.*

Mobile Bay was defended by several powerful forts. With Forts Gaines and Morgan at the harbor entrance in Union hands, the bay was effectively blockaded. The "breastworks" built by 161st New York Regiment were rough fortifications to protect Fort Morgan against attack from the landward side.

Mobile itself was protected by strong fortifications at Blakely and Spanish Fort, which were still in Confederate hands. Union commanders decided against attacking the city at this time, so Union regiments including 161st New York were ordered back to Louisiana.

The Union attack on Mobile Bay had diverted some Confederate troops who might otherwise have reinforced the defense of Atlanta, which was under attack by Major General William T. Sherman. The Confederates abandoned Atlanta on September 1.

> **THURSDAY, SEPTEMBER 1** *Laid in camp all day. Orders came to move at 6 o'clock PM. In the morning got a letter from home.*
>
> **FRIDAY 2** *Went on fatigue work till 12 o'clock. Got our things, went on board the boat, laid the afternoon [and] all night.*

SATURDAY, SEPTEMBER 3, 1864 *Got the barge of[?] 11 AM. Stayed [until] 3 PM. Ran down to Fort Morgan. Stayed a spell, then ran over to Fort Gaines to put on rations.*

SUNDAY 4 *Started out at 3 o'clock AM. Ran out the Bay into the Gulf. A pilot came aboard. Entered the Mississippi at 6 o'clock PM.*

MONDAY 5 *Got to New Orleans at 6 AM. Tied up two hours, unhitched, ran up to put on coal. Laid there till night. Started out at 9 o'clock PM.*

TUESDAY, SEPTEMBER 6, 1864 *Ran all night and all day till 9 o'clock PM. Stopped three or four times through the day. Got off and laid on the ground without tents.*

The trip back to Morganza Bend, Louisiana was in the steamer *Kate Dale*. Chaplain William E. Jones remembered it as "an old blockade runner," and "the hottest and most uncomfortable 'transport' we have met with." Private Sylvester Retan wrote to his sister on September 7, "We were on the boat about 5 days and pretty hard up for rations." Private Hendrick Conrad died of typhoid during this trip. He was the son of Private H. A. Conrad, who preached on the ship in which William had sailed from New York less than six months before.

WEDNESDAY 7 *Orders to move down [the] bank a ways, then struck tents. Policed up the ground. Laid in camp the rest of the day. Wrote home.*

THURSDAY 8 *Wrote to father Gleason. Laid in camp the rest of the day. Drew rations. The Tomas came in with two regiments [and] left them.*

William's "Tomas" was the transport *Thomas*. Father Gleason was his father-in-law, Lemuel Curtis Gleason.

THE WAR CONTINUES

SEPTEMBER 9–OCTOBER 9

By September 1864, the main action of the Civil War had moved east. Union strategy was to divide the Confederacy along a line from Chattanooga, Tennessee, through Atlanta to Savannah, Georgia. General Ulysses S. Grant planned to press the strongest Confederate armies hard and to grind them down. The Union blockade had cut supplies from outside the south. Texas, Arkansas, and western Louisiana were cut off by Union forces along the Mississippi River. The Confederacy was still fighting and its armies would continue to inflict heavy losses on the Union, but they could no longer win. What remained was for the Union armies to defeat them.

During the summer, Union troops had executed General Grant's grand strategy. Grant's army laid siege to the Army of Northern Virginia under General Robert E. Lee at Petersburg, south of Richmond. Another powerful Union army under Major General William T. Sherman captured Atlanta. Confederate forces in the west were not strong enough to make a major attack. The role of Union forces along the Mississippi River, including the 161st New York Volunteer Infantry Regiment, was to keep Confederate troops where they were and away from the War in the east. This required much sitting, and occasional chasing, but little fighting.

Officers of an army unit that is not fighting face a challenge. They must keep their troops busy enough to prevent boredom and discipline problems, while maintaining their readiness to fight. The 161st New York Volunteer Infantry Regiment was in camp at Morganza Bend, Louisiana. William Randall recorded drills, parades, and inspections in his day book, with occasional glimpses of the workaday routine by which he was fed, clothed, and sheltered.

FRIDAY, SEPTEMBER 9, 1864 *The regiment was on dress parade at 6 o'clock PM. Nothing very special today. Some drew clothes. James Pendergrass had the bilious colic.*

Private James Pendergast, age 29, enlisted on January 11, 1864, and was assigned to Company B. He survived his illness and was mustered out with the last members of the regiment on November 12, 1865.

SATURDAY 10 *Company drill in the morning. At 5 o'clock PM regiment battalion drill. Nothing very special in camp.*

SUNDAY 11 *I am on picket. Drew a pair of government shoes. No important news.*

MONDAY, SEPTEMBER 12, 1864 *Came in off of picket. Went on dress parade. Very warm. Made some biscuits. Baked them in brick oven.*

TUESDAY 13 *Company drill at 7 o'clock AM. Wrote a letter home. Went on battalion drill. Very warm today.*

None of William Randall's letters home have been found. Many letters did survive from other soldiers in the 161st New York Volunteer Infantry Regiment, including at least three collections and several individual letters. Soldiers wrote of their experiences in the Army, news of other soldiers, concerns about crops and livestock on the farms at home, reports of packages received and of what could be sent without spoilage, requests for socks and shirts made by sisters and mothers, and how money that they sent home was to be used or saved. A frequent request was for postage stamps, "as we cannot get them here." Soldiers were allowed to send mail by marking the envelope "Soldier's Letter" and having an officer or chaplain sign in place of the stamp. However, the recipient of such a letter had to pay the postage.

Soldiers did not usually report bad news to the folks at home because they wanted to spare their loved ones worry. A brief letter to his brother from Private Elihu M. Chamberlain, age 18, is typical:

Well Dick, how do you get along this Spring with the horses? I suppose you keep them fat and well. Write to me and tell me if they are going to have any colts or not, and all about things up there. Well, I must stop till next time, so good-bye from EMC to LeEC.

In a post script to a younger brother, he added,

Charley, How do you do? I think you are a big boy by this time. Well, write me a letter and tell me about the lambs and calves and the steers, too. Well, I must stop so good bye from your brother.

Private Chamberlain enlisted and mustered in to Company I on January 14, 1864. He and his brothers lived in Smithfield Township, Bradford County, Pennsylvania. His letter was written from University General Hospital in New Orleans on May 10, 1864. He had been admitted to the hospital on April 10 suffering from intermittent fever and diarrhea. He died on June 5, 1864.

A letter written by Private Cornelius Osterhout to his mother on September 27, 1864, is exceptional because he mentions his poor state of health.

I was glad to hear that you [are] all well. I cannot say that I am well. I have had the diarrhea pretty bad. I have fallen away fifty pounds in three weeks. I haven't strength enough to lift a pail of water, but I think I will get over it in a week or two. You said that Gebin[?] had started back. I didn't think he would take much trouble to bring anything. If you all get a chance to send anything, I want some dried black raspberries and some dried cherries, some of the red kind, and a few currents. You needn't take any trouble with what you get. You choose. Anything [would] sure taste good to me.

Private Osterhout enlisted at Urbana (near Hammondsport), Steuben County, New York, on August 20, 1862, when he was just 16 years old. He was mustered in to Company A on October 27 and was given special service as a bodyguard because of his age. Soon after he wrote this letter he was sent home, where he died of chronic consumption on November 21, 1864.

WEDNESDAY 14 *Went out on company drill. Went on battalion drill at 5 o'clock PM.*

THURSDAY, SEPTEMBER 15, 1864 *Went on company drill at 7 AM, then on battalion drill in PM. Very hot and dry.*

FRIDAY 16 *Went out on dress parade at 7 AM. I am excused from drill today. No news of importance. Ordered to move in 15 minutes.*

A Union force was sent northwest from the camp at Morganza Bend toward Simmesport, Louisiana. Their primary mission was to gather food for men and horses, but the likelihood of being attacked by Confederate troops required a large force. During the night of September 16-17, Confederates captured some Union troops near Bayou Letsworth, about fifteen miles from Morganza Bend. They were pursued by Union cavalry. A brigade commanded by Colonel Joshua J. Guppey, consisting of 161st New York Regiment, 23rd Wisconsin, 75th and 92nd U.S. Colored Infantry Regiments, followed cavalry and Confederates. The Confederates escaped across the Atchafalaya River, so Colonel Guppey gave up the chase and returned to Morganza. William remained in camp and did not accompany his regiment.

SATURDAY 17 *Regiment started going out. Heavy cannonading this morning. Out on today's excursion.*

SUNDAY, SEPTEMBER 18, 1864 *Regiment came in this forenoon at 10 o'clock AM. They had a hard march, captured some rebels, had a little fight. Some killed on both sides.*

MONDAY 19 *Laid in camp all day. Regiment inspections at 1/2 5 o'clock PM [4:30].*

TUESDAY 20 *Laid in camp all day. Fixed our guns up for inspection. At 9 o'clock PM ordered to march at 11 o'clock.*

WEDNESDAY, SEPTEMBER 21, 1864 *We started on the march to the Chaplio River. Started at 1 o'clock AM. Marched 20 miles and camped on the Chaplio. At 8 o'clock AM struck tents.*

William's "Chaplio" is the Atchafalaya River.

TUESDAY 22 *Some went across the river foraging, got sweet potatoes, meat of all kinds, and everything you can think of.*

FRIDAY 23 *Ordered to march in an hour. Then we started 8 o'clock AM. Got in camp at 4 o'clock PM back at Morganza.*

SATURDAY, SEPTEMBER 24, 1864 *Laid in camp all day. Nothing very special news. Got a mail from home. Went on dress parade at 5 o'clock PM.*

Army hospital records showed that William was admitted on September 25 with fever and returned to duty on October 6, but his day book entries do not agree.

SUNDAY 25 *Was ordered to go out on inspection. A very fine day. At 5 o'clock PM went out to drill.*

MONDAY 26 *Went on dress parade 7 o'clock AM, then laid in camp till 5 o'clock PM, then a battalion drill.*

TUESDAY, SEPTEMBER 27, 1864 *They had dress parade 7 o'clock AM, then laid in camp till 5 o'clock PM, then had battalion drill.*

WEDNESDAY 28 *They had dress parade at 7 o'clock AM. I made sour biscuit baked in a brick oven, then had a battalion drill at 5 o'clock PM.*

THURSDAY 29 *They had dress parade 7 o'clock AM, then drilled the awkward squad, then had battalion drill at 5 o'clock PM.*

William's mention of additional drill for the awkward squad (or "ancord squad," as he spelled it) may mean that he was assigned to it.

FRIDAY, SEPTEMBER 30, 1864 *They had dress parade at 7 AM, then drilled the awkward squad at 9 o'clock AM and at 3 PM, then battalion at 5 o'clock PM.*

SATURDAY 1 *We laid in camp till 5 o'clock PM, then they had dress parade, the awkward squad drilled at 9 o'clock AM.*

SUNDAY 2 *The regiment inspection at 8 o'clock AM, then company G. Two of the boys had a fight.*

MONDAY, OCTOBER 3, 1864 *Expected to have a drill. Laid in camp all day. Just at sundown had marching orders to pack up.*

TUESDAY 4 *Got knapsacks and formed a line at 5 o'clock AM so they did and started to march at 6 AM down to Bayou Cares.*

The *Official Record* states that 161st New York Regiment went to Bayou Sara. William remained on guard in the camp at Morganza Bend instead of accompanying them.

WEDNESDAY 5 *Came off camp guard this morning. Laid in camp all day. The regiment came back after dark from Bayou Cares.*

THURSDAY, OCTOBER 6, 1864 *Orders to fix up for knapsack inspection. Went out and formed a line at 5 o'clock PM.*

FRIDAY 7 *Laid in camp all day till 4 o'clock PM, then company drill, then dress parade at 5 PM.*

SATURDAY 8 *Laid in camp all day till 2 o'clock PM, then we went out on dress parade. Very cold night.*

SUNDAY, OCTOBER 9, 1864 *We were ordered out on knapsack inspection. Very warm day.*

CHASING CONFEDERATES
(October 10–November 8)

Confederate forces along and west of the Mississippi River were not strong enough to mount a major campaign, but they kept the Union Army busy with raids and guerrilla actions. On October 10, 1864, the 161st New York Volunteer Infantry Regiment was sent up to Union Point, where Confederates were reported to be moving cattle across the river. The expedition found neither enemy troops nor cattle.

MONDAY 10 *Went on camp guard at 10 o'clock AM. Ordered to brigade inspections at 11 AM. Ordered to march aboard the boat. Started up the river.*

TUESDAY 11 *This morning found ourselves up the river some 50 miles. Ran across the river. The boys went foraging at night. Marched 3 miles.*

WEDNESDAY, OCTOBER 12, 1864 *Started at 6 o'clock AM, marched through the woods till 1 1/2 o'clock PM. Went 18 miles. Laid 2 or 3 hours, marched back about 8 miles and camped.*

THURSDAY 13 *Started at 4 o'clock AM. March 10 miles. Got to the boats [at] 8 o'clock AM. Went on board. Started up the river. Stopped at Natchez 1 hour, started out up the river.*

FRIDAY 14 *A tug boat hitched on to run up a ways. Our boat jammed it against the bank and it broke in two and sank. Got to Vicksburg at 12 o'clock. Orders to stay 8 hours in camp on shore.*

SATURDAY, OCTOBER 15, 1864 *Went on board at sundown and started up the river. Ran all night, all day.*

SUNDAY 16 *Stopped twice in the night for fog. Then we ran all the forenoon and till 2 o'clock PM. We landed at White River Landing, then we went in camp. Put up tents.*

MONDAY 17 *Was fixing up camp. Got orders to pack up for a march. Stayed in camp the rest of the day.*

Union commanders rightly feared Confederate Major General Nathan Bedford Forrest and his cavalry. Troops under General Forrest had captured Fort Pillow, Tennessee, in April 1864 and had slaughtered most of the 600 defenders, about half of whom were ex-slaves in U.S. Colored Regiments. In June, in Mississippi, General Forrest defeated a Union force nearly twice as large as his own. In August, his cavalry paraded through Memphis, which was nominally under Union control. General Sherman wrote, "Forrest is the very devil."

In October, General Forrest's cavalry forces were reported to be along White River in Arkansas, then along the Mississippi at Memphis, then as far north as Columbus and Paducah, Kentucky. In fact, he had sent raiders toward Paducah to divert attention from his main force in western Tennessee. 161st New York Regiment was ordered to Columbus, but William was left behind in Arkansas. He did not rejoin his regiment until November 13.

TUESDAY, OCTOBER 18, 1864 *On picket today. At 4 o'clock AM the regiment went aboard. Started up White River. Came back at 12 o'clock. Order came the rebels were shelling Memphis. The troops and boats loaded down. Started up river.*

WEDNESDAY 19 *Came off from pickets. Only four of our company left. Regiment going up on boats all the time. Got a blouse coat.*

THURSDAY 20 *Wrote a letter home. News came that our regiment has gone to Ohio. Cold night, warm day.*

FRIDAY, OCTOBER 21, 1864 *Went on camp guard. Acted as corporal. No important news. Cold night. Ice in a water pail. Warm day.*

SATURDAY 22 *Got relieved at 8 o'clock PM. Had a very cold night, middling warm day. No important news.*

SUNDAY 23 *Laid in camp all day. We don't know where the regiment is for certain. Cold night, quite comfortable day.*

MONDAY, OCTOBER 24, 1864 *Went on camp guard today. No news of importance, only that the rebels have made a dash into Morganza Bend.*

TUESDAY 25 *Was relieved this morning. Got two letters from home, one dated the 18 of October.*

Soldiers who were captured in the Battle of Sabine Cross Roads were paroled in October 1864, after six months in Confederate custody. When paroled, a soldier returned to his own side under a personal pledge to not take up arms again until he was properly exchanged. Such pledges were honored by the men who made them and respected by their comrades. Prisoners were exchanged at the rate of sixty privates for a general, fifteen for a colonel, four for a captain and two for a sergeant.

Many soldiers who were captured early in the War were quickly paroled or exchanged. After General Grant became General in Chief of the Armies of the United States, exchange of prisoners was mostly stopped. Returning prisoners had become the largest source of men for the Confederate Army, more than new recruits or returning sick and wounded. The Confederacy badly needed men who were in Northern prison camps, while the Union could afford to leave some of its soldiers in Southern prisons.

WEDNESDAY 26 *Laid in camp all day. Wrote a letter home. It rained quite hard.*

THURSDAY, OCTOBER 27, 1864 *Finished a letter home and sent it. No news of importance. Warm day and cold night.*

FRIDAY 28 *Laid in camp all day. Cut my foot. Got a letter from home. Some of the men voted today and sent their votes.*

Nineteen years later, William claimed that he was growing lame because of an old injury from cutting his foot with an axe while gathering wood. He tried to get his pension increased and he submitted his diary to the U.S. Pension Board as evidence. There was no Army hospital record of the injury. His request for a larger pension was denied.

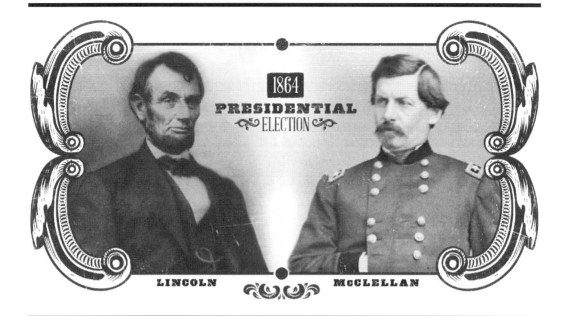

Many soldiers voted in the election of 1864, exercising their democratic right among "We, the People of the United States," to elect leaders of the government for which they were fighting. Soldiers who were 21 years old were voters and their votes were important in the presidential election. Hometown newspapers were carefully read and widely circulated through the 161st New York Regiment. Soldiers asked for them in letters to the folks at home. And newspapers in the Civil War era were politically partisan, not trying to give the appearance of neutrality like modern network television news. Opinions of publishers and editors were expressed with clarity and passion.

In the presidential election of 1864, Republican President Abraham Lincoln was re-elected with 55% of the popular vote. He carried most of the states and defeated the Democratic candidate, Major General George B. McClellan. General Sherman's victories in Georgia helped Lincoln's cause.

Because he was separated from his regiment, William did not get to vote.

> **SATURDAY 29** *Laid in camp all day. No news of importance. Only it is very rainy and mud aplenty.*
>
> **SUNDAY, OCTOBER 30, 1864** *Laid in camp all day. There isn't important news that I know.*
>
> **MONDAY 31** *Laid in camp all day. Only we drew ten days rations, some flour, some salt fish.*

TUESDAY. NOVEMBER 1 *Stood camp guard and was taken down with the Sumerplaint. Run me quite hard.*

"Summer complaint" was diarrhea, even when it occurred in November.

WEDNESDAY, NOVEMBER 2, 1864 *I am in good deal of pain today. We had orders to get ready to go to the brigade and then it was countermanded and we stayed.*

THURSDAY 3 *I am no better today. Quite [a] misery. It doesn't rain very hard but cold. No important news.*

FRIDAY 4 *About the same. I am not any better. No news from the regiment yet.*

SATURDAY, NOVEMBER 5, 1864 *I feel a little better today. I sold my dress coat. No news about camp. Bright sunshine and warm.*

SUNDAY 6 *I am very weak today. Feel a little better at sundown. No important news. A fine day.*

MONDAY 7 *We laid in camp all day. No important news, only 76 Illinois Regiment went up White River. Am not much better.*

TUESDAY, NOVEMBER 8, 1864 *Feel a little better today. Laid in camp all day. Quite rainy. Very windy now here.*

PREPARING FOR WINTER
(November 9–December 31)

The American Civil War was mostly fought in warm weather months. Armies went into winter quarters like great hibernating beasts. Soldiers concentrated on trying to stay warm. Private William Randall was still at White River Landing, Arkansas, separated from his regiment, which had gone to Columbus, Kentucky.

WEDNESDAY 9 *Our major came to us this morning to get transportation. Gave us orders to pack up for the first boat.*

"Our major" was Willis E. Craig, second in command of 161st New York Regiment. He was mustered in at Elmira on October 27, 1862, as Captain of Company H. He was promoted to Major on September 16, 1863, when he was 26 years old.

THURSDAY 10 *Laid in camp all day waiting for a boat. Nothing important going on.*

FRIDAY, NOVEMBER 11, 1864 *We were ordered to pack up for the boat. Marched aboard at 2 o'clock PM and started up the Mississippi River.*

SATURDAY 12 *Ran all night till 12 o'clock. At noon got to Memphis. Laid till 6 PM, started out.*

SUNDAY 13 *Ran all night, all day till 5 o'clock PM. Landed here at Columbus, Kentucky. Went up on the hill to camp [with] the regiment.*

MONDAY, NOVEMBER 14, 1864 *Got 4 letters from home and wrote one home. Went downtown, then laid in camp all day. About 30 new recruits to our company.*

The arrival of new recruits meant that William Randall was no longer among the newest men in Company K. Now he was a veteran with some experience to pass along to the new men.

TUESDAY 15 *Went on picket this morning. No news of importance.*

WEDNESDAY 16 *Got relieved this morning. Came in camp. It [is] rainy now. Fixing up camp.*

THURSDAY, NOVEMBER 17, 1864 *Went on picket and it rained all day and all night. No news of importance.*

FRIDAY 18 *Got relieved this morning and it rained and [is] very muddy. Helped build a tent.*

SATURDAY 19 *Went on camp guard. Laid with our straps on all night in fear of the rebels.*

SUNDAY, NOVEMBER 20, 1864 *Was relieved at 11 o'clock AM. Laid in camp the rest of the day. A very fine day. Wrote a letter home.*

MONDAY 21 *Went on picket. Very cold and [it] snowed a little. Ground is frozen soon. Fatigued [from] standing on post.*

TUESDAY 22 *Got relieved this morning and it snowed a little. Very cold day.*

WEDNESDAY, NOVEMBER 23, 1864 *Stayed in camp all day. Fixed over our tent. Put one bunk a top of the other. I was very tired.*

THURSDAY 24 *Was detailed to go on picket. A fine day. I am on post now. No news of importance today.*

FRIDAY 25 *I was relieved this forenoon. The news is that the pay rolls have come and I signed them. Wrote a letter home.*

SATURDAY, NOVEMBER 26, 1864 *Stayed in camp all day. Plenty of camp stories. The pay master has coin. Orders to pack up everything but tents.*

Pay masters usually paid troops with paper money. Being paid with gold and silver coins was unusual.

William's pay included part of his enlistment bounty. As a three-year volunteer he was entitled to $300 from the Federal government, which was paid at a rate of $20 per month. The state of New York also paid a $75 bounty to a volunteer, which William left with his wife Cynthia at home. (An 1864 dollar was equivalent to $13.56 in 2010.)

> **SUNDAY 27** *This morning I was detailed to go on picket and on inspection. Heavy marching orders. Got a letter from home.*
>
> **MONDAY 28** *Was relieved this morning. Got paid $150 dollars. Struck tents at 12 o'clock noon. Stayed in line till 4 o'clock PM, then march on the boat. Moved down the river, broke the rudder blade [and] tied up.*

General Forrest's Confederate cavalry had returned to Mississippi so 161st New York Regiment was ordered to Memphis, Tennessee. On December 5 they were ordered back to White River Landing, Arkansas, as part of Fourth Brigade, Reserve Corps, Military Division of West Mississippi. They did not reach White River until December 20th.

> **TUESDAY, NOVEMBER 29, 1864** *Started out this morning, steered by another boat. Stopped at night.*

Private Sylvester Retan wrote to his sister about this voyage:

> *We started and got about a mile from Columbus and the rudder of the boat broke and we tied up and waited until a boat came along and towed us down to Memphis. We did not start until the next morning and at daylight started. All went well until just at dark the other boat broke loose from us and left us drifting down the river. The boat swung around in the river and on we went downstream until we came to a bend in the river. Then the boat swung around and went broadside against the bank. The hands jumped ashore and managed to get a tow line out and tied her up and we lay there until morning. We put out blankets and in the morning the other boat took us in tow again and everything went all right the rest of the way. There were two regiments on board. The name of this boat is the Baltic.*

> **WEDNESDAY 30** *Started out down the river. Landed at Memphis at 3 o'clock PM. Marched through town, out a mile, and camped.*
>
> **THURSDAY, DECEMBER 1** *Stayed in camp and altered the line for tents. Went down town. Express $130 dollars home. Got a letter from home.*

In a letter to his parents dated April 4th, 1864, Private George C. Coleman wrote, "A mail has just this minute arrived at the chaplain's tent and the joyful shout, 'Mail! Mail! Mail!' has gone through camp like an electric spark."

> **FRIDAY, DECEMBER 2, 1864** *Went to work on our tents. Got it up and laid the boards in it. There is flu reported.*
>
> **SATURDAY 3** *Stayed in camp all day. Finished our tent. Laid on our bunks tonight.*
>
> **SUNDAY 4** *I was detailed on camp guard. Had some prisoners for not being at roll call.*

One duty of the camp guards was to watch soldiers who were imprisoned as penalty for some offense or breach of discipline. Being absent from roll call was a minor offense but it might be punished with time in the guard house if it was repeated.

In a letter to his sister dated March 5, 1863, Corporal Samuel Adams Johnson of the 161st New York Regiment wrote this story of guard duty and roll call:

> *Oh, I must tell you a good one about George. Every time any one in the company is absent from roll call they are put on extra duty such as Regimental or Brigade guard. George missed one or two mornings in succession and was put on guard so after that he thought he would tire them out. (By the by, guard duty is not as hard as picketing.) So every morning he would get up, clean his belts and brasses, pay no attention to roll call, but when the drum beat for guard mounting he would fall in and take his place. He did so for five mornings. At last the orderly asked him what he was doing there. He said he was going on guard. The orderly asked him who told him to. He said no one, only he was not up at roll call and he supposed of course he was on. He [the orderly] told him he might go to his tent (George). I thought you would get tired at last. He has not been on guard since.*

Corporal Johnson, age 28 years, enlisted at Elmira on August 14, 1862, and mustered into Company C. He was wounded in action at Donaldsonville, Louisiana, on July 13, 1863. The wound took his right leg, which had to be amputated. Then it took his life. He died on July 30, 1863, at Baton Rouge. When he wrote this letter there were four privates named George in his company.

Routine for the regiment in camp at Memphis was much the same as it was in other camps along the Mississippi River. They did not leave the camp at Memphis for White River Landing until December 17.

MONDAY, DECEMBER 5, 1864 *Got relieved this morning. Wrote part of a letter home. Went out on a brigade review. Warm weather.*

TUESDAY 6 *Company drill four hours in a day. Got letter from home. Fine weather. Got camp tents up.*

WEDNESDAY 7 *Squad drill half hour, company drill half an hour AM, PM two hour brigade drill.*

THURSDAY, DECEMBER 8, 1864 *Squad drill in AM one hour, company drill one hour AM, regiment drill PM two hours. Very cold weather.*

FRIDAY 9 *Snow or hail this morning. Very cold and stormy. No drill today. Ice on the ground is an inch deep.*

SATURDAY 10 *No drill today. Rubbing up our brasses for a review. Brigade inspection and review.*

SUNDAY, DECEMBER 11, 1864 *The review is countermanded today. Very cold day. Stayed in camp all day.*

MONDAY 12 *Went out on squad drill one hour, company drill one hour AM, Company drill one hour PM. Ordered to pack up.*

TUESDAY 13 *We [are] packed up. Ready to strike tents. Stayed all day in camp. Received two letters from home.*

WEDNESDAY, DECEMBER 14, 1864 *Camp guard 90 odd men. We were ordered to pack up tents and be gone. The order was countermanded for a few days. Fixed up again. Dress parade. On camp guard.*

THURSDAY 15 *Got relieved this morning. Stayed in camp all day. Had dress parade at 4 o'clock PM. All quiet.*

FRIDAY 16 *Laid all day long in readiness to strike tents at any time. Ninety odd men for camp guard.*

SATURDAY, DECEMBER 17, 1864 *Order to strike tents torn up. Stayed till 3 o'clock PM. Marched through the mud to the boat. Had to burn some of the boards.*

SUNDAY 18 *Got a letter from home. Stayed here all day and it rained all day long. Very heavy fog.*

MONDAY 19 *This morning we started down the river. Very cold rain and very hard rain. Went on guard. Tied up. Stayed all night.*

TUESDAY, DECEMBER 20, 1864 *Started at 5 AM, ran all day, got to White River Landing at 5 PM. Stayed on the boat all night.*

WEDNESDAY 21 *March off at 7 AM, camped, then sorted out our tent boards. Put up our tents. Cold but clear.*

THURSDAY 22 *Went on camp guard. The boys started a mud chimney. Very cold. Thawed a little at noon.*

FRIDAY, DECEMBER 23, 1864 *Got relieved at 9 AM. A very little warmer today. Had a salute of thirty-five guns for [General] Thomas's Victory. Warm day.*

The Union Army of the Cumberland under Major General George H. Thomas defeated the Confederate Army of Tennessee under Lieutenant General John B. Hood on December 15-16 south of Nashville. Hood's army retreated south into Alabama. They were no longer an effective force.

SATURDAY 24 *Laid in camp all day. Fixed up our guns for inspection. Quite a warm day. Very muddy today.*

SUNDAY 25 *Were in camp today. It rained. Very muddy. Wrote a letter home. Had a very good time today. Christmas.*

The last two pages of William Henry Randall's day book are barely legible. His service as a private in the 161st New York Volunteer Infantry Regiment continued into 1865, but he did not continue to keep a diary.

MONDAY, DECEMBER 26, 1864 *Stayed in camp. [The rest is illegible.]*

TUESDAY 27 *[Mostly illegible] got back at 8 PM.*

WEDNESDAY 28 *Was on guard all night. Got relieved at 7 AM. Had a chicken for dinner. Stayed in camp all day.*

THURSDAY, DECEMBER 29, 1864 *[Mostly illegible] night the cavalry camp on the [?] and to [?].*

FRIDAY 30 *Our company is ordered on picket. The river is rising very fast. Cold rain tonight.*

SATURDAY 31 *Was relieved this morning at 8 1/2 AM. Went in camp. Fixed up for inspection.*

A New Year and Another Journey

JANUARY 1–FEBRUARY 28, 1865

The last entry in William Henry Randall's day book is for December 31, 1864. He did not have a day book for 1865. Muster reports in his pension file show that he was present with his company from November 1864 through February 1865, and was wounded on March 31, 1865, during an attack on Spanish Fort, near Mobile, Alabama.

In the absence of a day book, other records show where William went and what he did. *The History of the 161st New York Volunteers*, published by Chaplain William E. Jones in October 1865, Private John Merwin's 1902 *Roster and Monograph*, letters from other soldiers in the regiment, and *The Official Records of The War of the Rebellion*, all provide information to reconstruct the regiment's actions.

As 1865 began, the Confederacy was beaten but not broken. Union forces held New Orleans, Baton Rouge, Natchez, Vicksburg, Little Rock, Memphis, Nashville, Chattanooga, Atlanta, and Savannah. Richmond and Charleston were under siege. But the Confederate government still commanded large armies that continued to fight against Union efforts to defeat the rebellion.

Confederate Lieutenant General John Bell Hood's Army of Tennessee had been defeated in December while attacking Nashville. They withdrew into Alabama, where they continued to worry Union commanders. Union Major General Edward R.S. Canby, commanding the Military Division of West Mississippi, gathered his forces and planned an attack into Alabama by way of the Gulf Coast.

THURSDAY, JANUARY 5, 1865: 161st New York Volunteer Infantry Regiment and William Randall were ordered from Devall's Bluff, along the White River in Arkansas, to "proceed without delay to New Orleans."

SUNDAY, JANUARY 8, 1865: The regiment embarked in the steamboat John H. Dickey and headed down river. Along the way, Confederate guerrillas fired at them. The boat was struck several times but there were no casualties. In the night they passed the cotton boat Venango, which had been set on fire by guerrillas.

MONDAY, JANUARY 9: The John H. Dickey stopped at Vicksburg for coal, then sailed at 5 p.m. At 7 p.m. they collided with the steamboat John Raine. Dickey's pilot house was wrecked and the port side near the bow was badly damaged. Men were injured and others leaped overboard to try to swim ashore. The John Raine stayed alongside the damaged Dickey, took the troops aboard, then carried them to their destination. Casualties from the accident were three drowned and twenty-three injured; two of the injured men later died. This accident caused greater loss to 161st New York Regiment than any action against the enemy since the Battle of Sabine Cross Roads.

WEDNESDAY, JANUARY 11: The regiment arrived at Kenner (also called Kennerville), Louisiana, a few miles up the Mississippi River from New Orleans.

FRIDAY, FEBRUARY 3, 1865: 161st New York Regiment was assigned to Third Brigade, First Division, XIII Corps, under Colonel Loren Kent of Illinois. Combined strength of the 161st New York, 29th Illinois, and 30th Missouri Regiments at Kenner was about 1,600 men. 23rd Wisconsin Regiment was also assigned to Kent's Brigade but had not yet arrived from White River, Arkansas.

THURSDAY, FEBRUARY 9: In a letter to his sister, Private John Wesley Bush of Company I wrote:

We have been expecting to move every day for some time but do not know where we will go to. It has been hot weather all this month. It has rained every day but one, but it looks as if we would have a fine time now. There is not much news here. They begin to talk of peace commissioners being sent to Washington from the rebel states but I do not believe a word of it, but hope it is time if they expect to settle at all. Some seem to think that we will go to Mobile. We move every month but that will play out in a few months with me. They have been offering $1500 for men to enlist in the regulars for five years and if it was not for father and the rest of you I would go, but I think I had better stay my time out and then take care of father and be with you. I think he needs me worse than old Abe and I had rather live with him.

Private Bush added this bit of news: "There was a steamer run on a bar a few days since, a few rods below here, and sprung a leak and sank so as to cover the boilers, but no one hurt nor lost. She had no troops on her. Her name was the **Otis Hall**. She was a fine boat but is good for nothing now."

SATURDAY, FEBRUARY 11: 161st New York Regiment travelled in rail cars to New Orleans, then marched north to Lakeport on Lake Ponchartrain.

MONDAY, FEBRUARY 13: The regiment boarded the steamer Planter and sailed for Mobile Bay.

WEDNESDAY, FEBRUARY 15: Arrived at Dauphin Island, Alabama. Chaplain Jones wrote that the Planter sailed by way of Lake Ponchartrain, Lake Borgne, Mississippi Sound, and Grant's Pass.

WEDNESDAY, FEBRUARY 22: Chaplain Jones wrote that Washington's birthday was celebrated with a prize drill in the morning (won by Company G) and athletic sports in the afternoon. He also reported an increase in spiritual concerns: "The hospital tent was fitted up with seats, and, in addition to regular Sabbath services, prayer meetings were held every evening, and a greater degree of religious interest was manifested in the Regiment than ever before."

TUESDAY, FEBRUARY 28, 1865 161st New York Regiment was with the rest of Third Brigade, First Division, XIII Corps, at Dauphin Island, Alabama, west of the main entrance to Mobile Bay, between the bay and the Gulf of Mexico. 23rd Wisconsin Regiment had joined the Brigade. Brigadier General James C. Veatch commanded First Division and Major General Gordon Granger commanded XIII Corps.

A NEW CAMPAIGN
(March 17–April 1, 1865)

General Canby was in overall command of Union forces at Mobile Bay. His orders from Union Army Headquarters stated that his objective was Selma or Montgomery, Alabama, including the capture of Mobile if he thought it necessary. His army was reinforced with divisions from the Army of the Cumberland, but foul winter weather slowed travel and gave the Confederates time to strengthen their defenses. It was mid-March before General Canby assembled all his forces. He planned to attack Mobile from the east, to either capture the city or to force its evacuation.

When the Mobile Campaign began on March 17, Major Willis E. Craig commanded 161st New York Regiment. Lieutenant Colonel William E. Kinsey, their former commander, had replaced Colonel Kent as commander of Third Brigade, First Division, XIII Corps.

William Kinsey joined the Union Army on April 30, 1861. He enrolled at Bath, Steuben County, New York, as a Corporal in Company A, 23rd New York Volunteer Infantry Regiment. He was promoted to First Sergeant of Company A on May 16. (William Randall's cousin, Ellis, was a Private in Company D.) 23rd Regiment was assigned to the defenses around Washington, D.C., until March 1862, when they joined the campaign in northern Virginia. Kinsey's ability was recognized and rewarded. On September 3, 1862, he was appointed First Lieutenant and Adjutant of the new 161st New York Regiment. On July 14, 1863, when he was 26 years old, he was promoted to the rank of Lieutenant Colonel, New York Volunteers, over older and more senior officers of 161st Regiment.

The *Official Record* contains reports and journals of Lieutenant Colonel Kinsey and Major Craig, which provide an outline of what 161st New York Regiment and William Randall did in the Mobile Campaign.

FRIDAY, MARCH 17, 1865: Third Brigade broke camp on Dauphin Island and embarked in transports for Navy Cove, on the east side of the entrance to Mobile Bay.

SATURDAY 18: At 2 o'clock a.m., the Brigade landed at Navy Cove and bivouacked on the beach. At 9 a.m. they formed into line and marched four miles on the Gulf shore road. Then they camped on sand hills near the Gulf.

SUNDAY 19: Reveille at 4 a.m. Third Brigade formed a line at 7 a.m. and marched east on Telegraph Road toward Dannelly's Mills. At noon they forded Little Lagoon and halted for an hour while the wagon train crossed. They bivouacked at night, having marched twelve miles.

MONDAY, MARCH 20, 1865: The Brigade marched at 6 a.m. After going seven miles, they came to a swamp through which the train of artillery and supply wagons could not move on the mucky road. They bivouacked while a fatigue party from 30th Missouri Regiment repaired bridges and rebuilt corduroy road. Heavy rain began soon after they made camp.

TUESDAY 21: Cold rain continued until 3 p.m. Fatigue parties continued work on the road.

WEDNESDAY 22 The Brigade struck tents and marched at sunrise (about 6 a.m.). They went about two miles, and found the roads impassable in sections that had not been repaired. The Brigade stacked arms, spread out along the road, cut trees, laid corduroy, lifted and hauled and dragged and pushed wagons and cannons out of the muck. At 8 p.m. they went into bivouac, having advanced only four miles.

THURSDAY, MARCH 23, 1865: At 6 a.m. the Brigade marched two miles, then halted while rations were distributed, then marched two more miles and made camp. The entire Brigade was assigned to build corduroy roads to allow wagons to pass. The work was finished at midnight.

FRIDAY 24: Third Brigade marched at 5:30 a.m. along the North Branch of Fish River toward Dannelly's Mills. The road was good. They crossed Fish River on a pontoon bridge at noon and camped two miles beyond the crossing. Lieutenant Colonel Kinsey wrote, "Had good camping ground on a high, dry ridge. Weather very fine."

SATURDAY 25: Third Brigade marched north at 2 p.m. behind Second Brigade. They marched only four miles and went into bivouac at 6 p.m. 161st New York Regiment furnished three officers and 200 men for picket duty.

SUNDAY, MARCH 26, 1865: Third Brigade was ordered to march at daylight but did not move until 8 a.m., behind Second Brigade. The march was slow and irregular. They were on a good road except when crossing two streams with very high banks, where there was much delay in getting wagons across. They marched eight miles, to within 1-1/2 miles of Spanish Fort at 3 p.m. First and Second Brigades were formed in line of battle, and Third Brigade in reserve formed a line about 100 yards behind them. There they remained until evening, when 161st New York Regiment was ordered forward to support the First Brigade picket line. Companies A, B, D, and G were later ordered to relieve the skirmish line.

MONDAY 27: Major Craig reported, "The enemy made a dash on the picket line at 7 a.m., but was repulsed. Companies A and D were engaged in the skirmish. The regiment was moved up in support of the picket line, which was advanced as skirmishers." The movement toward Spanish Fort covered "very rough and broken ground" in the pine woods. After advancing about a half mile, they came into a clearing in front of the fortifications where they engaged Confederate skirmishers. They pushed forward under cover of a ravine to a position about 1,200 yards from the main fortification. "In the afternoon I rejoined the brigade, which was moved forward and joined General Slack's brigade (First) on the right and directly in front of Spanish Fort. The four companies alluded to above remained on the skirmish line until dark. The casualties were two men wounded, one of whom was erroneously [reported] killed." At 10 p.m. a fatigue party of 150 men, including 60 men from 161st New York Regiment, was sent to the front line to dig rifle pits.

The two men who were wounded were Private Christopher C. Such, Company A, age 21, and Private Frank L. Thurston, Company D, age 30. Private Thurston died of his wounds on June 5 in a hospital at Greenville, Louisiana. Private Such survived and was mustered out with 161st Regiment on October 17. He is identified as one of the wounded in a list of casualties in Chaplain Jones's history.

Union artillery began to shell Spanish Fort with 53 siege guns and 37 field guns. They kept at it for twelve days. Each gun was fired every three minutes during the day and every thirty minutes at night.

TUESDAY 28: 161st New York Regiment was sent to the rear to build a bridge across D'Olive's Creek and to repair roads and bridges leading to Starke's Landing.

WEDNESDAY, MARCH 29, 1865: After the bridge was completed, the Regiment was ordered by General Canby to report for duty to Brigadier General Joseph Bailey at Starke's Landing, where they stood picket, guard, and provost duty around the army's supply base. They did not rejoin Third Brigade until April 10.

An intense 24-hour bombardment of Spanish Fort began on Friday, April 7. On April 8 at 5:30 p.m., Union troops entered the fort. By midnight they captured it, after most of the remaining Confederate defenders fled to Mobile.

Meanwhile, a Union column under Major General Frederick Steele had laid siege to the Confederate fort at Blakely, Alabama, five miles north of Spanish Fort. Fort Blakely surrendered on April 9. Confederate Major General Dabney H. Maury withdrew his remaining forces from Mobile on the night of April 11, before the city was attacked. Union forces, with 161st New York Regiment in the lead, marched into Mobile the next day.

Men were wounded and killed in the battles for the forts that protected Mobile, and their sacrifice had no effect on the War's outcome. General Ulysses S. Grant wrote in his *Memoirs*, "I had tried for more than two years to have an expedition sent against Mobile when its possession by us would have been of great advantage. It finally cost lives to take it when its possession was of no importance."

A letter written by Private Sylvester Retan to his sister on April 4, 1865, from Starke's Landing, Alabama, states this:

Our army is around a little fort called the Spanish Fort and the Johnny Rebs are on the inside. We were at the front the first day and helped drive them into their works. That was a week ago last Monday [March 27]. We fought them all day. One got wounded in Co. A...C.C. Such, a slight wound. Since then William Prentiss met with rather bad luck. He got hurt by the explosion of a torpedo [a land mine]. He has gone to Fort Gaines to a hospital. We, the 161st, are in an Engineer Brigade under General Bailey, the same man we were under last summer.

Private Prentiss was mustered out September 8, 1865, at Elmira. He had the bad luck to be the last casualty in the 161st New York Regiment before the War ended.

WILLIAM RANDALL GOES HOME

SATURDAY, APRIL 1, 1865: William Randall's pension records show that he was sent to the general hospital at Fort Gaines with a gunshot wound through the left hand.

SUNDAY, APRIL 2 – TUESDAY, MAY 9, 1865: William Randall was at General Hospital, Fort Gaines, Alabama.

MONDAY, MAY 15 – SUNDAY, MAY 28, 1865: William was at Barracks General Hospital at New Orleans, Louisiana.

MONDAY, MAY 29 – TUESDAY, JUNE 6, 1865: He was on board the transport Northern Light. This same ship had carried the 161st New York Volunteers from New York City to New Orleans in December 1862 when they were a new regiment on their way to the War along the Mississippi River. Now the ship was taking home some of the regiment's injured veterans.

TUESDAY, JUNE 6, 1865 William Randall was admitted to White Hall Military Hospital, Bristol, Pennsylvania, suffering from a gunshot wound of the left hand. He was incapable of performing the duties of a soldier because of injury to his left hand, and he was rated 3/4 disabled. This was later reduced to 1/3 disabled. He had a total loss of the third finger of his left hand and loss of flexure in the ring finger.

WEDNESDAY, JUNE 21, 1865 Private William Randall was discharged from the U.S. Army at White Hall Military Hospital.

William signed an affidavit in November 1865, which stated that he suffered a gunshot wound through the left hand in a skirmish with the enemy at Starke's Landing, Alabama. The *Official Record* states that 161st New York Regiment was sent to Starke's Landing on March 28, 1865, but it contains no mention of skirmishes there. A hospital record states he was wounded on April 1. He was at the hospital at Fort Gaines from April 1 – May 9. Fort Gaines was about three hours by boat from Starke's Landing. A pension application dated May 14, 1866, states William was wounded "on the first day of April, 1865, in front of Mobile in skirmish line in front of Spanish Fort State of Alabama."

THE WAR ENDS
(after April 1, 1865)

On April 9, at Appomattox Courthouse, Virginia, Confederate General Robert E. Lee surrendered the Army of Northern Virginia to General Grant. General Lee's surrender has come to be remembered as the end of the American Civil War, but it was almost two more months before all other Confederate forces surrendered. Brigadier General Joshua L. Chamberlain was selected to receive the surrender of weapons by the Army of Northern Virginia. He described the experience in his book, ***The Passing of the Armies***. As each unit approached to surrender their arms and flags, his troops saluted and were saluted in return. The surrender was a meeting of soldiers who respected one another, one army honorably defeated, the other victorious, after long struggle. The salute was not planned as part of a ceremony. General Chamberlain did it because it was the right thing to do.

But despite the respect of opposing soldiers for one another, the War ended with a death shudder that doomed the possibility of forgiveness, a generous armistice, and genuine peace. On April 14, in Washington, President Abraham Lincoln was murdered while attending a play with his wife. He died early the following morning. The evil of the President's assassination began very quickly to work its poison.

On April 17, near Raleigh, North Carolina, Lieutenant General Joseph E. Johnston surrendered his army to Major General William T. Sherman. General Johnston signed an armistice covering all remaining Confederate forces, and General Sherman gave him generous terms. The terms had been discussed three weeks before with President Lincoln and General Grant. General Sherman's armistice allowed the rebels to keep their property. It did not occur to him that, for Southerners, property included slaves. In the bitter aftermath of Lincoln's murder, the terms of surrender were rejected by Secretary of War Edwin M. Stanton, who accused Sherman of treason and demanded harsher conditions. General Grant intervened to calm the situation. General Johnston signed a more severe surrender document on April 26.

General Chamberlain wrote of learning of the murder of President Lincoln, and of his concern that the troops would take things into their own hands and seek revenge on the defeated people around them. A memorial service for the President was held for General Chamberlain's troops in Virginia. Union commanders in Mobile were less successful in restraining their men.

Private John Merwin's ***Monograph*** told how troops at Mobile responded to news of President Lincoln's murder:

The army was stricken dumb, but when reaction set in the men were in a rage that almost defied discipline. Paroled Confederate prisoners were still wearing their uniforms, but for the most part were discreet in action and speech. A few who were indiscreet soon paid the penalty, a thrust of the bayonet or a shot from the revolver silenced all unfavorable remarks. A number were killed after the first few days the news was received. The feeling against the Confederate gray culminated in an order from the Commanding General requiring the Confederates to remove the gilt buttons and all insignia of rank from their clothing.

On May 4, Lieutenant General Richard Taylor surrendered the remaining Confederate forces in Alabama, Mississippi, and eastern Louisiana. Confederate President Jefferson Davis was captured at Irwinsville, Georgia, on May 10.

On May 25, an ordnance warehouse in Mobile exploded while Confederate powder and shells were being moved there. The explosion destroyed the northeast quarter of the city and killed about 500 people. Some members of the 161st NYVI were injured in the explosion.

The 161st New York Regiment sailed in late May from Mobile in the transport *N.P. Banks*, to Fort Barrancas, Florida, at the mouth of Pensacola Bay.

Confederate units in Shreveport, Louisiana, surrendered on May 26. The Union Army finally took Shreveport, the objective of the Red River Campaign in which William Randall's War experience began. All remaining Confederate forces west of the Mississippi River were surrendered on June 2.

On May 31, the 82nd U.S. Colored Regiment and 161st New York Regiment left Fort Barrancas for Apalachicola, Florida. They sailed in the transports *Peabody, N. P. Banks, Clyde, Hussar,* and *Tampico*. Colonel Ladislas Zulavsky commanded the combined force. They were to watch for guerrillas and outlaws, maintain order, supervise cotton shipments, and serve as an occupation force in the territory of a defeated enemy.

The 161st New York Regiment was transferred at the end of July to Fort Jefferson, Florida, seventy miles west of Key West in the Dry Tortugas. They relieved the 110th New York Regiment, who were about to be discharged. On September 20, soldiers of the 161st Regiment whose enlistments were about to expire were mustered out. Most of these men had enlisted when the regiment formed in 1862. They had survived three years of war. The rest of the regiment, those who joined later as replacements, were formed into Companies A and B of the 161st New York Infantry Battalion. Men from Company K were transferred to Company A.

On September 25, 348 veterans embarked in the transport *Thomas A. Scott* and sailed for home. After stops at Key West and Hilton Head, they reached New York City on October 6. On the 7th they returned to Elmira, to the barracks where they were organized three years before. On October 12 the citizens of Elmira gave them a reception and a dinner with speeches. On the 17th the enlisted men received their pay and were discharged. The officers were paid and discharged the next day. That evening, they joined in a farewell dinner.

On November 12, 1865, the last two companies of the 161st New York Volunteers were discharged and mustered out of service at Tallahassee, Florida.

Farragut and Granger after the Battle of Mobile Bay.

PILGRIMAGE II

Stephen and Pete resumed their Civil War pilgrimage on April 12, 2004. They got underway at 8 a.m. from Stephen's home in the Uptown neighborhood of New Orleans, for Mobile Bay, Alabama. Stephen drove east on Claiborne Ave, then out of the city on I-10. As he drove, Pete read aloud from his notes about Private William Randall in the Mobile campaign of 1865. William had crossed Lake Ponchartrain and Mississippi Sound with the 161st New York Volunteer Infantry Regiment in the steamboat *Planter*; Stephen and Pete rode across the lake on a long causeway.

North of Lake Ponchartrain, the interstate highway took them across the flat marshes of southern Mississippi at 65 miles per hour. They stopped at the Alabama Welcome Center, where a helpful attendant gave them a map showing Civil War sites and campaigns around Mobile Bay.

The Union Army and Navy made two campaigns against Mobile. The first, in 1864, included the famous naval Battle of Mobile Bay in which Admiral David Farragut said, "Damn the torpedoes! Full speed ahead!" (or words to that effect). Forts at the mouth of Mobile Bay were captured in the 1864 campaign, allowing the Union Navy to close the port to blockade runners. The 161st New York Regiment went to Mobile Bay in September 1864 but they did no fighting. The second campaign was launched in 1865.

Stephen and Pete left I-10 at the town of Grand Bay. Alabama route 193 took them across the Grant's Pass entrance to Mobile Bay, on a four-mile causeway to Dauphin Island. William Randall had arrived there with his regiment in February 1865. This was where the 161st New York Volunteers waited to begin the second campaign against Mobile. Like them, the pilgrims saw bright sunshine reflected from the water, along with white sand, seashells, gulls, and other shore birds. Where Union Army troops once covered the island with tents, there were now restaurants, shops, real-estate offices, and vacation homes.

Dauphin Island was much like other barrier islands that Pete and Stephen knew well. Their family had visited the Outer Banks of North Carolina many times. Stephen first played in warm ocean surf and sand before his second birthday. Before William Randall travelled to Mobile Bay at age 37 in 1864, he had never seen an ocean beach or a barrier island.

Fort Gaines was at the eastern end of Dauphin Island. The pilgrims paid $10 each to enter. The Union Army and Navy paid much more dearly to enter Fort Gaines on August 7, 1864. Brochures explained the Battle of Mobile Bay, in which the fort was bombarded by Union Navy monitors and forced to surrender. Fort Gaines and Fort Morgan, at the mouth of Mobile Bay, were equipped with old-fashioned smooth-bore cannons. They were out-gunned by rifled naval guns of Admiral Farragut's ships. A souvenir map of Fort Gaines showed where a shell from the monitor *U.S.S. Chickasaw*, which was firing from inside the bay north of the fort, struck inside the south wall.

Pete asked a tour guide, who was dressed as a Confederate soldier, where the Union Army hospital had been located. He said that the Confederate hospital was located outside the fort, but he did not know if the Union hospital was also there. William Randall was at the Union Army hospital at Fort Gaines from April 1 until May 9, 1865, waiting for his wounded left hand to heal.

The Confederate hospital was on a site now filled by the "Estuarium," which contained plants and animals from the Alabama estuary and tidelands. In 1865, a camp for several thousand Union soldiers had covered much of the eastern end of Dauphin Island near Fort Gaines. The guide said that beach erosion around the fort was a serious problem. The shore-line, which was across a road below the east wall of the fort, had been a half mile farther away during the Civil War.

The Mobile Bay Ferry took Stephen and Pete across three miles of salt water to Fort Morgan. On the boat they got out of the car to enjoy the sea breeze and birds, which flocked to people who fed them. William Randall would have seen shore birds when he was in Mobile Bay. They were much different from the birds he knew from his farm home in the upper Susquehanna River Valley.

Three miles south, outside the bay, was Sand Island Lighthouse. The tall brick structure Pete and Stephen saw was built in the 1870s, a golden decade of American lighthouse construction. It was built to the same plans as the lighthouse at Corolla, North Carolina, which Pete and Stephen had climbed several times. On Sand Island,

Confederate troops blew up an earlier lighthouse in 1863. When William Randall crossed Mobile Bay in 1864 and 1865, a temporary wooden structure was on Sand Island, only forty feet tall, visible about seven miles.

To the north, the bay was full of oil rigs and their tender boats. Pete paid a toll when they left the ferry. He remembered his wife Judy's joke that a bridge or ferry toll was a bargain, because it would be a long way to swim towing the car.

Leaving the ferry, they almost missed the entrance to Fort Morgan, on the east side of the main entrance to Mobile Bay. The ticket seller noted their Pennsylvania license plate, and said she was a second great-granddaughter of Union General Gordon Granger. He commanded XIII Corps, to which William Randall was assigned in the Union Army's second Mobile campaign.

Fort Morgan was a shore artillery base until World War II. Most displays in the museum and fort were about more recent history than the Civil War. There was a display about Admiral Franklin Buchanan, who commanded Confederate Navy forces in the Battle of Mobile Bay. He was an early Commandant of the U.S. Naval Academy at Annapolis, from which Pete had graduated in 1961. A display about storms said that Navy Cove, where the 161st New York Regiment landed on August 24, 1864, and again on March 18, 1865, had disappeared in a hurricane in the early 20th century.

After Union forces captured Fort Morgan, the next strong points defending the city of Mobile were Spanish Fort and Fort Blakely. The map from the Alabama Welcome Center showed the route followed by Union Army XIII Corps. From Fort Morgan it led east along Alabama route 180, on a spit of seashells and sand. The modern paved road followed the shell road on which William Randall marched on March 18, 1865, with the 161st New York Regiment.

South of the road across Little Lagoon, which had to be forded in 1865, were large homes and apartment buildings of the community of Gulf Shores. On September 16, 2004, five months after Stephen and Pete visited, Hurricane Ivan stormed across this spit of sand with 110 m.p.h. winds and a twelve-foot tidal surge. The storm opened a channel from the ocean into Little Lagoon. It destroyed many buildings at Gulf Shores and in Florida communities to the east.

Where the coastal barrier sand spit met the mainland, the XIII Corps route turned north. The map showed Oyster Bay, where William Randall wrote in his day book, "Orsters aplenty." (He was what Pete's father called a "fearless speller.")

Across the route where XIII Corps moved cross-country in March 1865, the map showed county roads on a neat surveyor's grid. Portage Creek was channeled into a wide canal. What was forest and marsh in 1865 had become farms, a gravel pit, and housing developments. But the route where Union Army troops cut trees to build a corduroy road appeared still to be woodland. South of the Fish River Crossing was Dannelly's Mills, which had become a marina.

Modern development filled the bay-side retirement towns of Fairhope and Daphne. At a Daphne city park the pilgrims looked across the bay, to tall modern buildings of the city of Mobile. Starke's Landing, where 161st New York Regiment was assigned when William Randall was wounded on April 1, 1865, was a half mile north of the park. Long rows of pilings stretched into the bay. They marked the Union Army base where supplies and ammunition were unloaded for the siege.

To the north were Spanish Fort and Fort Blakely. They were built of earth and timber, not stone, brick, and concrete like Forts Gaines and Morgan. Spanish Fort had been turned into a suburban housing development, but Blakely was now an Alabama State Park. The entrance attendant supplied a map. Except for road grading, the battlefield was little changed from the way Confederate troops defended it in 1865. Dirt roads led to where the map showed Union lines. A recent fire had burned away ground cover.

At Fort Blakely, the pilgrims stood where Civil War soldiers stood, and saw terrain and earthworks like the soldiers saw. Dense forest blocked long views. The nearby Tensaw River could not be seen from the battlefield. Pete thought about digging trenches and fighting in that forest, under the random roar of cannon fire and exploding shells, which could drive sanity from a man's mind.

From Fort Blakely they drove to the housing development on the site of Spanish Fort. An overgrown ravine looked like it might have looked in 1865, but most of the area was a wooded residential neighborhood. Markers on some streets told of nearby regiments and fighting. Markers also warned homeowners that the yards were full of iron shell fragments and lead Minié balls.

Spanish Fort was captured by Union troops on April 8, 1865. Fort Blakely was taken on April 9, the same day that General Robert E. Lee surrendered the Confederate Army of Northern Virginia at Appomattox Courthouse, Virginia. Confederate troops abandoned Mobile on April 11. The 161st New York Volunteer Infantry Regiment marched proudly into the city on April 12, but Private William Randall was not with them. He was at the hospital at Fort Gaines.

What is it about the American Civil War that causes people to dress in old-style clothes, to hand-sew flags, to re-enact marches, battles, and encampments? Why did Dr. Eugene Poinboeuf arrange to be buried on the site of a battle, and to erect stones that told its story? Why do states set up commemorative areas, parks, and historic markers, and publish modern maps showing details of the War? Why did Stephen and Pete make pilgrimages to places where their ancestor marched, camped, fought, and was wounded?

The American Civil War was the most important experience in the lives of the people who fought it, and of their families. It shaped them, and our nation's history. The War was terrible for everyone who endured it. The pain, loss, and grief that it caused are still deep scars in our history. At the War's end, residents of the Confederate South struggled with their defeat, and residents of the Union North rejoiced in victory. Their joy was brief. Then they mourned the murder of President Abraham Lincoln, whom many had grown to love.

The Civil War recalls the most intense feelings of the American experience. To honor the memory of those who endured the War, we try to understand what they suffered, and to share what we can of their feelings.

We Honor Their Memory

A gunshot wound cost William Henry Randall most of the use of his left hand. He was considered to be one third disabled, so he received a one third pension. A full pension was "half pay," so William received 1/3 of 1/2 of the $16 pay of an Army Private, or $2-2/3 per month. The monthly amount was increased to $4 in 1875 and to $6 in 1882. (The initial $2-2/3 pension would be worth about $38 in 2010 dollars; $4 in 1875 would be worth $77 in 2010; $6 in 1882 would be about $132 in 2010.)

When William Randall returned home from the War in the summer of 1865, he was thirty-eight years old. His son Truman was eight, Ida was six, and Albert turned two that summer. Bertha Jane would have been four if she had lived. In the following years, William and Cynthia Randall had four more children. William A. was born April 24, 1866. Curtis followed two years later, May 5, 1868. He was named for a grandfather and an uncle, both called Curtis Gleason. Another daughter, Clarinda Eunice, was born January 16, 1871, and Anna arrived on July 18, 1873.

On New Years Day, 1877, Truman Randall married Sally Josephine Peterson, whose father was also a Union Army veteran and Bradford County farmer. It was a double wedding, with Sally's sister Ida marrying Truman Lindsley on the same day. Son George Henry Randall, named for both his grandfathers, was born on February 3, 1878. George and his cousin Bertha Thetgee (daughter of his mother's sister Charlotte Peterson Thetgee and Robert Thetgee), who was born just two days before, were the first grandchildren of the next generation. Truman and Sally Randall farmed in Ridgebury Township, Bradford County, Pennsylvania, near their parents.

In the spring of 1879, at age 13, William A. Randall died. He was buried near his sister Bertha, in the Dutchtown Cemetery at Wilawana, Bradford County, Pennsylvania, near Orcutt Creek and the Chemung River. The cemetery was not far from the family home, where his parents still farmed. Eleven years later, in 1890, the census taker found William H. Randall, age 64, still living near Wilawana.

Loss of the use of his left hand was a grave disability for a man who supported his family by farming. The aches and pains that William recorded in his day book continued to trouble him. He suffered through the rest of his life from pains in his stomach and belly. A photograph of him shows a man in pain. Rufus and Curtis Gleason, his wife Cynthia's brothers, reported in 1895 that he was often unable to work because of the pain. Cynthia had to support him about half the time by taking in washing. Before 1897, William and Cynthia, and their daughter Clarinda, gave up farming and moved to Elmira.

As he neared the end of his life, William Randall and his family were proud of his Civil War service. Like other soldiers, his attitude changed through the War and after it ended. Many men enlisted with high moral values, a belief that righteousness and courage would win, and a clear goal of victory. But their ideals faded as they gained experience with the horrors of war. Hunger and cold led them to rob corpses and prisoners, and to take what they needed from civilians caught in the path of the armies. Survival became more important than victory. In the randomness of illness, injury, and death, they learned that survival seemed to be by luck. God did not protect those who were good. The righteous were as likely to die as those who gambled and swore. Major General William T. Sherman wrote what may be the best statement of how soldiers felt near the end: "I am sick and tired of war. Its glory is all moonshine. It is only those who have neither fired a shot nor heard the shrieks and groans of the wounded, who cry aloud for blood, more vengeance, more desolation. War is hell."

After the Civil War, soldiers who had gone to fight found that many who stayed home had prospered. Veterans organizations were formed to lobby Congress and state legislatures for adequate pensions, but they struggled for active members. For fifteen years the war experience was hidden. Perhaps it took that long for memories of horror to fade. Then the veterans organizations began to flourish, and high-minded attitudes returned.

A belief grew in the nation that War was noble sacrifice. Regimental histories were written. Generals published memoirs in which they verbally attacked their enemies and defended themselves. Statistical and historical summaries were compiled and published, lists of which regiments lost the most men in which battles. Popular histories with maps and sketches told again the stories of bravery and tragedy.

The *Official Records* were compiled and published in more than fifty volumes. Ink spilled more freely than blood, which may be a sign of progress in our American civilization.

Statistical summaries tell us that 161st New York Volunteer Infantry Regiment lost one officer and 55 enlisted men killed or died of wounds, and 250 died of disease and other causes. William Randall was one of 85 enlisted men and 7 officers who were wounded and survived. One officer and 42 enlisted men were captured and survived. Out of a total of 1,140 men who served in the 161st New York Regiment, William was among 441 casualties, 306 of whom died in service. A higher proportion of men died from disease in William's regiment than in the regiments of his cousins. He survived the War to live 33 more years and to die at home.

William Henry Randall died on September 20, 1898, at Elmira, New York. He was 71 years old. His sons Truman and Curtis purchased a lot in Elmira's Woodland Cemetery, where he is buried under a stone that identifies him as a veteran of Company K, 161st New York Volunteer Infantry Regiment. The lot is in the civilian section of Woodland Cemetery. Nearby is the military section with its neat graves of 3000 Confederate soldiers who died in Elmira prison camp. In death, victors and vanquished rest together.

William's widow Cynthia received a pension of $8 per month (about $204 in 2010 dollars) until her death seventeen years later, at age 78, on June 3, 1915. She was buried next to her husband. Her stone gives her maiden name, Cynthia Jane Gleason.

Cold stones in a cemetery and cold records in a file say little of the experience that earned the gratitude of our nation. William's day book was sent to the U.S. Pension Office in 1883 to justify his request for a larger pension, which was not granted. The little book has become a kind of magnifying glass through which to study the American Civil War.

For those who fought the American Civil War, it was the most important experience of their lives.

Near the end of his long life, Justice Oliver Wendell Holmes was asked what he thought was the most important thing he had done for his country. His career in the law included twenty years on the Massachusetts Supreme Court and thirty years on the United States Supreme Court. Among his judicial opinions are important and literate defenses of our fundamental rights of free speech and assembly.

But Justice Holmes's answer had nothing to do with the law. Instead, he said this: "Captain, Twentieth Massachusetts Infantry. Wounded three times, at Balls Bluff, Antietam, and Fredericksburg." His service to his country in the Civil War was the most important experience of his life. He is buried in Arlington National Cemetery, under an inscribed stone that puts his War service above his place on the U.S. Supreme Court. That was the way he saw it.

William's cousin Wesley Randall may also be buried at Arlington, in a mass grave of more than 2000 unidentified Union soldiers whose remains were recovered from the Virginia countryside around Manassas, where he died in the First Battle of Bull Run.

The American Civil War was the most important experience in the lives of the ten Randall and McDaniel cousins who served in the Union Army. The War took them far from home, put them under military discipline, put them close to other soldiers from all over the country. They saw sights and met people like they had never known in their upper Susquehanna Valley farms and towns. During the War they were hotter, colder, more hungry, more thirsty, more tired, more confused, and more frightened than they had ever been before or after. The War put them in danger of sickness and injury and death. It took the lives of two cousins and disabled four more. They saw men die in terrible ways. Those who escaped without physical injury had wounded memories.

These ordinary men who fought our Civil War, saved the United States of America. To them we owe the wholeness of our nation, the freedom of all its people, the integrity of our Constitution. "We the people," who govern ourselves by that unique agreement called the U.S. Constitution, must thank these ordinary men. Their sacrifice preserved our nation and bought the peace that we enjoy.

We honor their memory.

APPENDICES

ACKNOWLEDGEMENTS

This book came to be written because of Darcie Randall Ridolfi. She provided copies of the Civil War diary of William Henry Randall and of his pension records. She also sent copies of the pension records of the other Randall and McDaniel cousins. Another generous genealogist, Marilyn Scott Randall, provided a photo and the family tree of William Randall. They were generous with their help. "Acts of genealogical kindness" are typical of family history researchers.

Conrad Bush and Richard MacAlpine were also generous in sharing letters from men in the 161st New York Volunteer Infantry Regiment. Where William Randall's diary is terse, letters written by the three Retan brothers, by John Wesley Bush, and by other soldiers give more detail. Mr Bush was especially kind in sharing notes from his research and his transcriptions of newspaper articles relating to the 161st New York Volunteer Infantry Regiment.

One should not judge people based on their membership in a group, but librarians may be an exception. The author has almost always found them to be helpful. The work of librarians makes research like this possible. They responded to questions and requests with patience and promptness. One instance can stand for the class: Louise Arnold-Friend of the U.S. Army Military History Institute at Carlisle Barracks, Pennsylvania, guided the author to relevant resources in that wonderful institution. She also provided useable copies from microfiche of a book whose old pages were crumbling to dust.

Managers of Internet news group soc.history.war.us-civil-war moderated a forum that put the author in contact with other students of the American Civil War. They published a helpful reading list and "Frequently Asked Questions" with answers about the War. News-group subscribers also gave the author answers to several questions.

The Antioch Writers' Workshop at Yellow Springs, Ohio, also helped. Leaders of the opening sessions assured the author (as they assured every participant) that he was a writer, and told him to follow his passion. In the 2004 memoir workshop, Michael Dirda was especially encouraging. An early version of the Pilgrimage chapters was reviewed in the 2005 memoir workshop. It was improved by advice from Joyce Dyer, Amy Lemmon, Jean Silver-Isenstadt, and Rich Unger. The Letter from Home story was critiqued in 2005 in a prose workshop of the Writing Center at Chautauqua Institution. Comments from other participants, and from leader Philip Gerard, sharpened it. The book was also improved by editors Katherine Schilling and Stephen Schilling.

Photographs and maps in this book are from sources in the public domain. The Library of Congress web site was a valuable resource. Several images came from

The Photographic History of the Civil War. Maps were prepared from *The Official Military Atlas*. In making digital versions of these images available, Chester G. Hearn has done a helpful service for Civil War researchers and authors. Graphic designer Eric Yeamans selected and prepared the images, and laid out the book.

The book project hibernated for several years, during which the author wondered how to handle the Pilgrimage and Letter from Home material. The Centerville, Ohio, Public School System awakened it. Their seventh grade language and social studies curriculum requires a family heritage project. The author and his grandson, Christopher Buchheit, discussed the project, and Christopher decided to include his fourth great grandfather's diary in it.

This book is a history. Facts about Private William Henry Randall, his family, his regiment, and the American Civil War are, to the best of the author's knowledge, as he has written them. The Letter from Home does not survive. Its contents, and William's thoughts and words, are from the imagination of the author.

Like most writings about history, this book contains many opinions about what the truth might be. While the help acknowledged above has been essential, all errors of selection, interpretation, analysis, and conclusion are the author's alone.

SOME NOTES ABOUT SPELLING

Mark Twain is credited with the saying, "It is a poor mind that can find only one way to spell a word." He would have appreciated the spelling of William Randall.

Here is the original transcription of a page from Private William Henry Randall's Day Book. The headings were printed in the little book when William got it. Beneath them are his line breaks, spelling, and lack of punctuation and capitalization:

SATURDAY, APRIL 30, 1864

we was cald out
on musterd for
pay they comenst
damin the river
to get the gunbots
over the bar

SUNDAY, MAY 1

all quiete and pesible
and lovely to day
very warm in
dead out on in
spetion and a very
good metion

MONDAY 2

went out a forgi
on and made a
very good trip
but i was very
tierd all most
out

In this book, the page is interpreted as follows:

SATURDAY, APRIL 30 We were called out and mustered for pay. They commenced damming the river to get the gunboats over the bar.

SUNDAY, MAY 1 All quiet and peaceable and lovely today. Very warm indeed. Out on inspection, and a very good meeting.

MONDAY 2 Went out foraging and made a very good trip, but I was very tired [and] almost out.

William Randall's spelling, punctuation, capitalization, and grammar have been altered to conform to standard American English. Exceptions have been made for proper names, where William's spelling has been maintained in his day book entries and corrected in notes. To historians who object to these changes, the author apologizes. A copy of the original transcription can be supplied to anyone who requests it. The author hopes that other readers find the interpreted text more readable.

Similar changes have been necessary in a few of the letters of other soldiers. Conrad Bush performed a great labor in transcribing handwritten letters from his ancestor John Wesley Bush, and other soldiers' letters from pension files in the U.S. National Archives. The letters from Sergeant (later Lieutenant) Lewis E. Fitch were fine examples of the disappearing art of letter writing. Others needed varying amounts of editing. Readers who wish to read the original transcriptions can be put in touch with Mr Bush.

ABOUT THE ARMY

ARMY RANKS

Commissioned officers were ranked as follows, senior to junior:

Lieutenant General	
Major General	**All called Generals**
Brigadier General	
Colonel	
Lieutenant Colonel	
Major	
Captain	
First Lieutenant	**Called Lieutenants**
Second Lieutenant	

Enlisted men were ranked as follows, senior to junior:

- **Sergeant Major**
- **First Sergeant**
- **Sergeant**
- **Corporal**
- **Private**

Within each rank, seniority was by date of commission or promotion. The highest ranking officers in the Union Army were Major Generals until 1864, when the U.S. Congress approved one Lieutenant General, Ulysses S. Grant. The Confederate Army had several Lieutenant Generals.

A Rear Admiral in the Navy ranked with an Army Major General. A Navy Captain ranked with an Army Colonel.

The term "officer" is casually used to mean a commissioned officer. An enlisted man above the rank of Private is called a Non-Commissioned Officer.

ORGANIZATION OF THE UNION ARMY

Unit	Example	Usually Commanded by	Usually Consisted of
Army	Army of the Gulf	Major General	2 or more Corps
Corps	V, XIII, XIX	Major General	3 or more Divns.
Division	First, Second, Third	Major General	3 Brigades
Brigade	First, Second, Third	Brigadier Gen.	4 or more Regts.
Regiment	161st NY Volunteers	Colonel	10 Companies
Company	Company K	Captain	8 Squads
Squad		Sergeant	Corporal + 8-10 Pvts

Divisions within each corps and brigades within each division were simply numbered: First, Second, etc. Companies within each regiment were designated A through I and K. There was no J Company.

A battalion consisted of two or more companies that operated or maneuvered together. Companies of the 161st New York Volunteer Infantry Regiment were not permanently organized into battalions until after the War ended, when two reorganized companies were designated Companies A and B of the 161st New York Infantry Battalion.

Regiments were the fundamental units of permanent military organization. A Regiment might be assigned to different Brigades, Divisions, Corps, and Armies at different times through the course of the War. The strength of each regiment decreased as men were killed, wounded, captured, or lost to illness, desertion, or discharge at the end of their enlistment. From time to time, losses were replaced with new recruits. While the 161st New York Volunteer Infantry Regiment had about 800 men on its initial roster, and more than 1100 men served in the regiment during the War, effective strength for battle was not usually above 500 men. This was typical of Union Army regiments. Regiments in the Confederate Army were less able to find replacements for their losses.

GLOSSARY

adjutant (n) – an officer who is responsible for the correspondence of a commanding officer.

artillery (n) – (1) the part of an army that fights with guns that are mounted on carriages. (2) guns too heavy to be carried by hand.

barge (n) – a vessel that is towed or pushed by another vessel.

barracks (n) – one or more permanent buildings to house soldiers.

battery (n) – two or more cannons or mortars.

bayonet (n) – a pointed weapon that attaches to the end of a musket or rifle, which is used to attack the enemy with a thrusting motion.

bayonet (v) – to stab with a bayonet (n).

biscuit (n) – crisp dry unleavened bread in flat cakes; "hardtack".

bivouac (n) – a place where troops rest on the ground without shelter.

bivouac (v) – to rest in a bivouac (n).

blockade (v) – to cut off commerce by land and sea between an enemy and others; to close the seaports of an enemy.

blockade (n) – naval and land forces and operations to blockade (v) an enemy.

bluff (n) – a cliff with a broad, steep face.

breastwork (n) – a temporary fortification.

cable (n) – a strong, thick rope.

cannon (n) – a firearm on a fixed or moveable mount; any firearm too heavy or bulky to be carried or fired by hand.

cannonade (n) – a continuing repeated discharge of several cannon; a bombardment.

cannonade (v) – to subject a target to a cannonade (n).

canteen (n) – a small drinking flask for water or coffee. Each soldier carried one.

capture (v) – (1) to seize by force, surprise, or stratagem. (2) to gain a place held by an enemy.

casualties (n) – losses in numerical strength from death or wounds.

casualty (n) – a man who is killed or wounded.

cavalry (n) – the part of an army that marches and fights on horseback.

chaplain (n) – a clergyman who is responsible for the spiritual welfare of soldiers.

column (n) – a formation of troops with elements behind one another.

commissary (n) – a place or establishment where food is issued.

commissary (adj) – pertaining to an officer or non-commissioned officer with duties relating to the supply of food.

corduroy (n) – a road of logs that are placed across the direction of travel so as to prevent vehicles, animals, and men from sinking into mud.

deck (n) – a floor of a vessel on which one walks. (A vessel may have several decks above one another.)

dress coat (n) – a soldier's outer garment that is worn on special occasions and for dress parades.

drill (v) – to practice or to instruct in marching, military formations and movements, and skills in performing habitual duties, so as to inculcate and maintain discipline, control, and flexibility.

drill (n) – a session in which soldiers are drilled (v).

dysentery (n) – an infections disease marked by severe diarrhea with blood or mucous in the stool and inflammation or ulceration of the lower part of the bowels.

embargo (n) – an order prohibiting the sale or shipping of commodities, or the arrival or departure of ships.

engineer (n) – an officer with duties related to design and construction of forts, roads, railroads, bridges, machines, or weapons.

express (n) – a system for high speed special delivery of packages, money, or goods.

express (v) – to send by express (n).

fatigue duty (n) – an assignment to heavy labor for supply, upkeep, or construction. (Fatigue duty is performed without weapons.)

forage (n) – food for animals.

forage (v) – to collect food supplies for men or animals.

furlough (n) – a leave of absence for a stated period of time for an enlisted man.

guerrilla (adj) – pertaining to warfare by irregular troops who operate in more or less independent bands, and who fight by "hit and run" raids, avoiding pitched battles. (From a Spanish word meaning "little war.")

guerrillas (n) – irregular troops who engage in guerrilla (adj) operations.

gun (n) – (1) a firearm in general; (2) a firearm with a long barrel that is fired from a carriage or fixed mount..

gunboat (n) – a vessel that is armed with one or more guns.

infantry (n) – the part of an army that marches and fights on foot using rifles and bayonets.

inspection (n) – a critical examination to determine conformance to standards.

militia (n) – "citizen soldiers", troops employed and maintained by a state (rather than the national) government.

Minié bullet (n) – a conical bullet with a cavity at the base which is fired from a rifle. (Pronounced "minnie." A Minié bullet is heavier and faster than ball ammunition. Named for its inventor, French Army Captain Claude Minié.)

mortar (n) – a cannon with a short barrel that is fired at high angles of elevation so as to subject targets to falling shells.

musket (n) a smooth bore firearm that is fired from the shoulder.

parade (n) – a formal military ceremony with assembly or display of troops, usually with a march or procession.

parade (v) – (1) to assemble or move in a parade (n).

parole (n) – a pledge of honor by a prisoner to not resume fighting until properly exchanged.

parole (v) – to set a prisoner free after he has given his parole (n).

Parrott gun (n) – (1) a cast iron rifled cannon that is strengthened by shrinking bands or a sleeve over the rear part. (Invented by R P Parrott.) (2) a cast iron mortar with a steel tube lining the barrel.

picket (n) – a detachment of troops who are guarding a critical point; a sentry.

picket (v) – to guard as a picket (n).

picket line (n) – a guarded perimeter line around a camp where pickets (n) are posted.

police (v) – to pick up litter and trash; to clean up.

police duty (n) – an assignment to police (v) an area.

prisoner (n) – a person who is confined under guard.

private (n) – a soldier who holds the lowest rank.

provost (n) – a temporary prison.

provost duty (n) – a temporary assignment to guard prisoners or to enforce rules and regulations.

provost marshal (n) – an officer who is assigned to command military police or provost guards.

quarantine (n) – (1) an order setting up measures to prevent the spread of disease. (2) a place where a ship waits until port authorities determine that it has no communicable diseases on board.

quartermaster (n) – an officer with duties related to shelter, supplies, and transportation.

ration (n) – a prescribed allowance of different articles of food for the subsistence of one person or one animal for one day.

rear (n) – (1) in a battle, the direction away from the enemy or behind the body of troops who are fighting. (2) the direction opposite to the direction of movement. (3) that part of a force that comes behind.

rear guard (n) – a detachment of troops that follows the main body and gives it protection on the march.

reconnoiter (v) – to move over a possible field of operation in order to gather information about the terrain and the enemy.

regular (n) – a professional soldier.

reserve (n) – that portion of a body of troops that is kept in the rear or withheld from action at the start of a battle, with a view to being used to influence later action.

shell (n) – a projectile that contains explosive and a fuse for detonation, which bursts and scatters fragments.

shell (v) – to direct the fire of shells (n).

skirmish (n) – a combat between small forces or detachments of the main forces.

skirmish line (n) – a line of soldiers at extended intervals (several feet apart) in advance of the main line of battle.

torpedo (n) – a metal case containing explosive, which is placed below the surface of ground or water, and which is arranged so as to explode on contact. (Now called a contact mine.)

train (n) – (1) a line of wagons or gun carriages pulled by horses or mules. (2) a line of railroad cars pulled by a locomotive.

transport (n) – a vessel or train to move troops, equipment, and supplies.

volunteer (n) – a person who enters military service of his own free will, without compulsion. Opposite of a draftee. Not a professional soldier.

BIBLIOGRAPHY

Alotta, Robert I., *Civil War Justice: Union Army Executions Under Lincoln* (1991, Shippensburg, PA, White Mane Publishing Co.).

Records of executions, with discussions of some cases.

Boatner, Mark Mayo III, *The Civil War Dictionary* (1988, New York, David McKay Company, Inc.).

Summaries of campaigns and battles; biographies of general officers; notes about armaments, food, pay, strategy and tactics; .... An essential reference.

Bowen, Catherine Drinker, *Yankee From Olympus: Justice Holmes and His Family* (1945, Boston, Little, Brown and Co.).

Biography of Justice Oliver Wendell Holmes, Jr.

Bush, B. Conrad (editor), *Civil War Letters of John Wesley Bush* (Private communication from the editor, September 27, 1996).

Transcribed letters from Private John W Bush, Company I, 161st New York Volunteer Infantry Regiment, with notes about Private Bush, his family, other soldiers, and actions and history of the regiment.

Bush, B. Conrad (editor), *Civil War Letters From Pension Files in the U.S. National Archives of Soldiers of the 161st New York Volunteer Infantry Regiment* (Private communications from the editor, 1996-7).

Transcribed letters with notes about the following soldiers and their families: William M. Bell, Elihu M. Chamberlain, Charles M. Couch, Lewis E. Fitch, Charles H. Grieves, Thuel Hogancamp, Samuel A. Johnson, Orlando Barber, Cornelius Osterhout, Quincey D. Plaisted, Daniel Robinson, and James M. Snyder.

Bush, B. Conrad, *Newspaper Articles Relating to the 161st New York Volunteer Infantry Regiment* (Private communications, 1997).

Letters and articles from Bath, NY, *Steuben Farmers Advocate*, Elmira, NY, *Daily Advertiser*, Elmira, NY, *Press*, *The New York Herald*, The *New York Times*, and *New York Tribune*.

Catton, Bruce, *The American Heritage Pictorial History of the Civil War* (1960, New York, American Heritage Publishing Co.).

Summaries of some battles, campaigns, and the War. Many pictures.

Chamberlain, Joshua Lawrence, *The Passing of theArmies: An Account of the Final Campaign of the Army of the Potomac, Based upon Personal Reminiscences of the Fifth Army Corps* (1994, Gettysburg, PA, Stan Clark Books).

Personal history and nearly mystical remembering of the Appomattox Campaign, surrender of the Army of Northern Virginia, and Grand Review.

Davis, George B., Leslie J. Perry, & Joseph W. Kirkley; compiled by Calvin D. Cowles, *The Official Military Atlas of the Civil War* (2003, New York, Barnes & Noble. Reprint of 1891-5 folios).

Atlas to accompany the Official Records of the Union and Confederate Armies; beautiful maps.

Dyer, Frederick, *A Compendium of the War of the Rebellion* (Reprinted in 1979, Dayton, OH, Morningside Press, Vol. 2).

Concise summary of service of each regiment.

Fox, William F., *Regimental Losses in the American Civil War, 1861–1865* (1889, Albany, NY, Albany Publishing Co., reprinted in 1974, New York, Press of the Morningside Bookshop).

Statistical data about casualties.

Garber, Max, and Paul S. Bond, *A Modern Military Dictionary* (1942, Washington, D.C., Paul S. Bond Publishing Co.).

Helpful definitions of military terms.

Grant, Ulysses S., *Personal Memoirs* (1999, New York, The Modern Library imprint of Random House, reprint of 1885 edition).

Autobiography and authoritative report of the War.

Harper's History of the Great Rebellion (1866, New York, Harper's Publishing Co. Vol. 2).

Summaries of battles and campaigns with drawings and maps.

Johnson, Ludwell H., *Red River Campaign: Politics and Cotton in the Civil War* (1958, Baltimore, MD, The Johns Hopkins Press).

Comprehensive background and details of Red River Campaign, a valuable resource.

Joiner, Gary D, gen. ed., *Little to Eat and Thin Mud to Drink: Letters, Diaries, and Memoirs from the Red River Campaigns, 1863-1864* (2007, Knoxville, The Univ. of Tennessee Press).

Joiner, Gary Dillard, ***One Damn Blunder from Beginning to End: The Red River Campaign of 1864*** (2003, Wilmington, DE, Scholarly Resources Inc.).

Jones, William E., ***The 161st New York Volunteers*** (1865, Bath, NY).

The Chaplain's history of the regiment.

Joyous Coast Foundation, ***Images of America: Natchitoches*** (2003, Charleston, SC, Arcadia imprint of Tempus Publishing Inc.).

Linderman, Gerald F., ***Embattled Courage: The Experience of Combat in the American Civil War*** (1987, New York, The Free Press).

Study of soldiers' attitudes based on their letters and diaries.

MacAlpine, Richard S. (editor), "Civil War Letters: The Retan Boys of 'Old Steuben'", ***Fox Family History*** (1994 Summer issue).

Letters written by Anson, Nelson, and Sylvester Retan, Co A, 161st New York Volunteer Infantry Regiment.

McPherson, James M., ***Battle Cry of Freedom*** (1988, New York, Oxford University Press).

The single best history of the War.

McPherson, James M., ***For Cause & Comrades: Why Men Fought in the Civil War*** (1997, New York, Oxford University Press).

Systematic study of letters from 1071 soldiers.

Merwin, John W., ***Roster and Monograph: 161st Reg't N.Y.S. Volunteer Infantry*** (1902, Elmira, NY).

History and roster of the regiment.

Miller, Francis Trevelyan, & Robert S. Lanier, ***The Photographic History of the Civil War in Ten Volumes*** (1911, New York, Review of Reviews).

Many photographs. Available on CD.

New York Adjutant General's Office, ***Muster-in Rolls of N.Y. Volunteers*** (1866, Albany, Vol 4, pp. 531-551).

Muster-in rolls from 1862 of field and staff officers and of each company.

New York Adjutant General's Office, ***Annual Report for the Year 1904*** (No. 40, 1905, Albany, NY, Brandow, pp. 743-902).

Summary of service of each man who served in the 161st New York Volunteer Infantry Regiment.

Phisterer, Frederick (compiler), *New York in the War of the Rebellion, 1864–1865* (1912, Albany, NY, J.B. Lyon Co., 3rd Ed.).

Recruitment and financing of New York troops; brief history of each regiment, summary of service of each officer, and tables of losses in each regiment.

Richards, Caroline Cowles, *Village Life in America: 1852-1872, Including the Period of the American Civil War as Told in the Diary of a School-Girl* (1972, Williamstown, MA, Corner House Publishers).

Background of New York village life.

Sandburg, Carl, *Abraham Lincoln: The War Years* (1939, New York, Harcourt Brace & World, Inc.).

Background and political details from President Lincoln's view.

The Soldier in Our Civil War: A Pictorial History of the Conflict, 1861–1865 (1890, New York, Stanley Bradley Publishing Co.).

The War of the Rebellion: A Compilation of Official Records of the Union and Confederate Armies (1897, Washington, DC, Government Printing Office; Series I, Vols. 34 & 49).

The Official Records, reports and correspondence, battle and campaign reports of commanding officers.

U.S. Army Quartermaster's Department. *Roll of Honor: Names of Soldiers Who Died in Defence of the American Union* (Reprinted 1994, Baltimore, MD, Genealogical Publishing Co.).

Lists of soldiers who were buried in National Cemeteries.

PEOPLE IN THIS WRITING

People who are mentioned in this writing are identified below as Members of William Randall's family, as Officers and Soldiers, as Others, or as Members of the 161st New York Volunteer Infantry Regiment.

MEMBERS OF THE RANDALL FAMILY

Gleason, Curtis – brother-in-law, Cynthia's brother.

Gleason, Cynthia Jane – William's wife.

Gleason, Lemuel Curtis – father-in-law, Cynthia's father.

Gleason, Rufus B. – brother-in-law, Cynthia's brother.

Lindsley, Truman – husband of Ida Peterson Lindsley.

McDaniel, John – cousin, son of Aunt Orra Randall McDaniel. Served in 109th New York Volunteer Infantry Regiment. Died of typhoid pneumonia in hospital at Alexandria, Virginia.

Peterson, Charlotte – sister of Sally Josephine Peterson.

Peterson, George H – father of Sally Josephine Peterson, Truman Randall's wife.

Peterson, Ida – sister of Sally Josephine Peterson.

Peterson, Sally Josephine – daughter-in-law, wife of Truman Randall.

Randall, Albert – son, born July 4, 1863.

Randall, Andrew – cousin, son of Uncle Ichabod. Served in 90th New York Volunteer Infantry Regiment.

Randall, Anna – daughter, born July 18, 1873.

Randall, Bertha – daughter, born in 1863, died February 13, 1865, while William was away from home in the Army.

Randall, Clarinda Eunice – daughter, born January 16, 1871.

Randall, Curtis – son, born May 16, 1868.

Randall, Ellis – cousin, son of Uncle Freeman. Served in 23rd New York Volunteer Infantry Regiment. Wounded at Battle of Antietam.

Randall, Frederick – cousin, son of Uncle Freeman. Served in 27th New York Volunteer Infantry Regiment.

Randall, Freeman – uncle.

Randall, George Henry – grandson, son of Truman Randall and Sally Josephine Peterson Randall, born February 3, 1878.

Randall, Ichabod – uncle.

Randall, Ida – daughter, born October 8, 1858.

Randall, John – cousin, son of Uncle Rephah. Served in 137th New York Volunteer Infantry Regiment.

Randall, Levi – cousin, son of Uncle Ichabod. Served in 90th New York Volunteer Infantry Regiment.

Randall, Lyman – cousin, son of Uncle Rephah. Served in 64th New York Volunteer Infantry Regiment.

Randall, Nehemiah, I – William's grandfather.

Randall, Nehemiah, II – William's father.

Randall, Nehemiah, III – William's son, born June 24, 1854, died December 7, 1857.

Randall, Olive – aunt, wife of Truman Van Armburgh.

Randall, Orra – aunt, wife of Hiram McDaniel.

Randall, Rephah – uncle.

Randall, Truman – son, born August 17, 1856.

Randall, Wesley – cousin, son of Uncle Freeman. Served in 27th New York Volunteer Infantry Regiment. Missing and presumed killed in First Battle of Bull Run.

Randall, West – cousin, son of Uncle Rephah. Served in 137th New York Volunteer Infantry Regiment.

Randall, William A. – son, born April 24, 1866, died May 18, 1879.

Shaw, Electa A. Randall – younger sister.

Thetgee, Bertha – cousin of grandson George H Randall, daughter of Charlotte Peterson Thetgee and Robert Thetgee, born February 1, 1878.

Thetgee, Robert – husband of Charlotte Peterson Thetgee.

Van Armburgh, Truman – husband of Aunt Olive Randall.

OFFICERS AND SOLDIERS

More complete biographies of generals in the following list can be found in Mark Boatner's book, *The Civil War Dictionary*.

Bailey, Joseph – Union officer. Before the War he studied engineering in Illinois, then moved to Wisconsin where he was a lumberman. Joined the Army as Captain, 4th Wisconsin Cavalry, in 1861. He was a Lieutenant Colonel and Engineer Officer for XIX Corps in the Red River Campaign. Suggested and supervised construction of the dams that saved Admiral Porter's fleet. Promoted to Colonel, then Brigadier General, in 1864. After the War he was killed in 1867 while serving as sheriff of Newton County, Missouri.

Banks, Nathaniel P. – Union officer. Before the War he was a member of Congress, then Governor of Massachusetts. Appointed Major General when the War began. Commanded Department of the Gulf after 1863, including unsuccessful attacks on Port Hudson and unsuccessful expedition to the Sabine River. Commanded Union Army in Red River Campaign. Returned to Congress after the War.

Benedict, Lewis – Union officer. Attorney and politician. Appointed Colonel of 162nd New York Volunteer Infantry Regiment in August 1862 and led them in assault on Port Hudson. Killed in action at Battle of Pleasant Hill, April 9, 1864.

Canby, Edward R. S. – Union officer. West Point graduate (1839) and professional Army officer. Promoted to Major General in May 1864, and given command of the Military Division of West Mississippi. Led campaign against Mobile.

Chamberlain, Joshua L. – Union officer. Professor at Bowdoin College. Enrolled in August 1862 as Lieutenant Colonel, 20th Maine Infantry Regiment. Led them in Battles of Antietam, Fredericksburg, Chancellorsville, Gettysburg, Spotsylvania, and Cold Harbor. Wounded six times. Received Medal of Honor for action at Little Round Top in Battle of Gettysburg. Promoted to Colonel, then Brigadier General, he commanded two brigades and then First Division of V Corps. Received surrender of Confederate regiments of Army of Northern Virginia at Appomattox. After the War he served as Governor of Maine, President of Bowdoin College, Commanding General of Maine State Militia, President of Florida East Shore Railway. Died in 1914.

Dwight, William – Union officer. Commanded First Brigade, First Division, XIX Corps in Red River Campaign.

Emory, William H. – Union officer. Graduate of West Point (1831) and professional Army officer. Led First Division, XIX Corps, in Red River Campaign.

Farragut, David G. – Union officer. Professional Navy officer (became a Midshipman at age 9 in 1810). Commanded Navy forces against Port Hudson and Vicksburg. Commanded Navy forces in attack against Mobile Bay in August 1864.

Forrest, Nathan Bedford – Confederate officer. Cotton, land, livestock, and slave trader in Memphis before the War. Raised a cavalry battalion at his own expense in 1861. Wounded twice. Led raids against Union forces in Tennessee including Fort Pillow Massacre on April 12, 1864. After the War, he helped organize the Ku Klux Klan.

Franklin, William – Union officer. Graduate of West Point (1843) and professional Army officer. Commanded XIX Corps in the Red River Campaign. Wounded in the fight at Pleasant Grove (Battle of Sabine Cross Roads).

Gebin – Union soldier. Neighbor of Private Cornelius Osterhout's family who was home on leave in September 1864. Identity not otherwise known.

Gordon, George H. – Union officer. West Point graduate (1846) and lawyer. Commanded Army forces in attack against forts at the mouth of Mobile Bay in August 1864.

Granger, Gordon – Union officer. Graduate of West Point (1845) and professional Army officer. Commanded XIII Corps in 1865 in the Mobile Campaign.

Grant, Ulysses S. – Union officer. Graduate of West Point (1843), farmer, and merchant. Led Union forces in battles at Forts Henry and Donelson and at Shiloh, Vicksburg, and Chattanooga. Appointed General in Chief of the Armies of the United States in March 1864. Eighteenth President of the United States (1869-1877).

Guppey, Joshua J. – Union officer. Colonel, 23rd Wisconsin Infantry Regiment. Commanded Third Brigade, Second Division, XIX Corps, in summer of 1864.

Holmes, Oliver Wendell – Union officer. Enrolled in 1861 as Captain, 20th Massachusetts Infantry Regiment. Wounded three times, at Balls Bluff, Antietam, and Fredericksburg. Mustered out in 1863. Graduated from Harvard University Law School, and was a professor there before appointment to Massachusetts Supreme Court. Served more than thirty years on U.S. Supreme Court.

Hood, John Bell – Confederate officer. West Point graduate (1853) and professional Army officer. Wounded in Battle of Gettysburg. Commanded a corps, then Army of Tennessee, in defense of Atlanta in 1864. Led Confederate forces in unsuccessful Franklin and Nashville Campaign.

Johnston, Joseph E. – Confederate officer. Graduate of West Point (1829). Professional Army officer. Commanded Confederate forces at First Battle of Bull Run. Wounded twice at Battle of Seven Pines. Later commanded in the west, in defense of Atlanta, and in defense against General Sherman's Carolina Campaign.

Kent, Loren – Union officer. Enrolled in 1861 as First Lieutenant and Adjutant, 29th Illinois Infantry Regiment. Promoted to Colonel in 1863. Commanded Third Brigade, First Division, XIII Corps, at the start of the Mobile Campaign.

Lee, Robert E. – Confederate officer. West Point graduate (1829), professional Army officer, Superintendent of West Point (1852-55). Declined command of Federal Armies in 1861 and took charge of Virginia state troops. Commanded Army of Northern Virginia from 1862 until the end of the War. President of Washington College (now Washington and Lee University) until he died in 1870.

Maury, Dabney H. – Confederate officer. West Point (class of 1846) and professional Army officer. Commanded District of the Gulf.

McClellan, George B. – Union officer. Graduate of West Point (1846), professional Army officer, then Vice President of Illinois Central Railroad. Commanding General who organized and trained Union Armies in 1861 and 1862. Unsuccessful as a battlefield commander in Peninsula Campaign and at Battle of Antietam. Democratic candidate for President in 1864. Engineer and Governor of New Jersey after the War.

McMillan, James W. – Union officer. Enrolled in July 1861 as Colonel, 1st Indiana Artillery. Commanded Second Brigade, First Division, XIX Corps, during Red River Campaign.

Nims, Ormand F. – Union officer. Captain, Massachusetts Light Artillery, 2nd Battery (B), in Red River Campaign.

Pearsall, Uri B. – Union officer. Lieutenant Colonel, 5th Engineer Regiment, Corps d'Afrique, in Red River Campaign.

Pickett, George E. – Confederate Officer. West Point (class of 1846), professional Army officer and lawyer. Wounded in Battle of Gaines's Mill. In the Battle of Gettysburg, he commanded a Virginia infantry division which took part in the action that is now called Pickett's Charge.

Porter, David D. – Union officer. Professional Navy officer (became a Midshipman in 1829 at age 16). Commanded Mississippi Squadron. Commanded Navy fleet in Red River Campaign. After the War he served as Superintendent of Annapolis and Admiral of the Navy.

Sherman, William T. – Union officer. Graduate of West Point (1840), professional Army officer, then a banker and lawyer. Wounded in Battle of Shiloh. Commanded Department of the Tennessee, Military Division of the Mississippi, Atlanta Campaign, and Carolina Campaign. Commanding General of the U.S. Army from 1869 to 1883.

Sickles, Daniel E. – Union officer. U.S. Senator from New York before the War. Enrolled in June 1861 as Colonel, 20th New York Infantry. Commanded brigades and divisions, then III Corps in Army of the Potomac. Appointed Major General in 1862. Lost one leg in the Battle of Gettysburg.

Slack, James R. – Union officer. Lawyer and judge. Enrolled in December 1861 as Colonel, 47th Indiana Infantry Regiment. Led that regiment in the Red River Campaign. Commanded First Brigade, First Division, XIII Corps, in Mobile Campaign.

Smith, Andrew Jackson – Union officer. West Point graduate (1838) and professional Army officer. Commanded XVI Corps in Red River Campaign and in Mobile Campaign.

Smith, E. Kirby – Confederate officer. Graduate of West Point (1845) and professional Army officer. Commanded a brigade in First Battle of Bull Run, where he was wounded. Commanded Trans-Mississippi Department after February 1863. Defeated General Steele's Arkansas Campaign in 1864. Surrendered the last Confederate forces on June 2, 1865. President of University of Nashville (1870-1875).

Steele, Frederick – Union officer. Graduate of West Point (1843) and professional Army officer. Commanded Department of Arkansas in 1864, and led Arkansas Campaign. Commanded Military District of West Florida, and led column against Blakely in Mobile Campaign.

Taylor, Richard – Confederate officer. Son of President Zachary Taylor, brother-in-law of Confederate President Jefferson Davis, and Louisiana plantation owner. Defeated General Banks's Red River Campaign. Commanded Department of East Louisiana, Mississippi, and Alabama, which he surrendered on May 4, 1865.

Thomas, George H. – Union officer. West Point graduate (1840) and professional Army officer. Commanded Army of the Cumberland in Battles of Lookout Mountain and Missionary Ridge, in Atlanta Campaign, and in Battles of Franklin and Nashville.

Thompson, Cornelius – Union soldier. Farmer and probably a former slave. Private, Company A, 48th U.S. Colored Infantry Regiment. Convicted by general court martial on June 16, 1864, of murdering Miss Martha Richardson, a civilian laundress. Executed by firing squad at Vicksburg, Mississippi, on June 24, 1864.

Veatch, James C. – Union officer. Lawyer and public official. Enrolled in August 1861 as Colonel, 25th Indiana Infantry Regiment. Commanded First Division, XIII Corps, in Mobile Campaign.

Zulavsky, Ladislas – Colonel of 82nd U.S. Colored Infantry Regiment in Mobile Campaign. Commanded occupation force at Apalachicola, Florida, in summer of 1865.

OTHERS

Chamberlain, Charley – Younger brother of Private Elihu Chamberlain.

Chamberlain, Dick (LeMC) – Brother of Private Elihu M. Chamberlain.

Chase, Salmon P. – Lawyer, U.S. Senator, Governor of Ohio, U.S. Secretary of the Treasury (1860-1864). Resigned to accept appointment as Chief Justice of the Supreme Court.

Davis, Jefferson – Graduate of West Point (1828). Served for seven years as professional Army officer, then became a Mississippi plantation owner. Returned to the Army in War with Mexico and was severely wounded. Served in Congress, as U.S. Senator, and as Secretary of War. President of the Confederate States of America (1861- 1865). Led the Confederacy through the Civil War.

Fairman, Charles – Friend of Sergeant (later Lieutenant) Lewis E. Fitch.

Lincoln, Abraham – Lawyer and politician. Sixteenth President of the United States (1861-1865). Led the Union through the Civil War. Assassinated on April 14, 1865.

McPherson, James B. – Historian, author, and professor at Princeton University. Authority on the American Civil War.

Richardson, Martha – Civilian laundress who was murdered by Private Cornelius Thompson in June 1864.

Stanton, Edwin M. – Lawyer. U.S. Attorney General (1860), Secretary of War (1862-1867).

Taylor, Zachary – U.S. General whose leadership won the War with Mexico (1847). Twelfth President of the United States (1849-50). Died in office. Father of Richard Taylor, father-in-law of Jefferson Davis.

Truman, Harry S. – Farmer, merchant, politician, U.S. Senator. 33rd President of the United States (1945-1953). Issued order to end segregation in the U.S. Armed Forces.

Underhill, A. L. – Editor of the Bath, New York, *Steuben Farmers Advocate*. Recipient of letters from John Little.

MEMBERS OF THE 161ST NEW YORK VOLUNTEER INFANTRY REGIMENT WHO ARE NAMED IN THIS WRITING

A note about places where soldiers enlisted:

When the 161st New York Regiment was organized in August 1862, officers travelled throughout the legislative district around Elmira, and men enlisted near their homes. Later in the War, when replacements were being recruited, men were enlisted under town names to satisfy quotas for those towns. (Towns were criticized for lack of patriotism if it was necessary to draft men to meet their quotas.) Men from Bradford and Tioga Counties in Pennsylvania travelled to Elmira to enlist. Bounty payments were higher there than in Pennsylvania.

Bradford and Tioga Counties, Pennsylvania, are just a few miles south of Elmira and Corning, New York. During the Civil War, it was much easier to travel north to Elmira than south to places in Pennsylvania where regiments were recruited. South of Bradford County, one now finds "World's End State Park" in the "Endless Mountains." The area deserves those names. Bradford and Tioga Counties still have closer ties to the Southern Tier of New York than to Pennsylvania. Many family names in the following list can be found in the 1860 census in Bradford and Tioga Counties, Pennsylvania.

For each soldier in the following list, this data is shown: name, age when enlisted, date of enlistment, place of enlistment, company, rank when mustered in, date mustered in, reason why the soldier left the regiment, rank when he left, date when he left, place where he left, and notes. Reasons for leaving the regiment are abbreviated as follows:

Died - Died of disease or of wounds.
Dis - Discharged for disability.
Drown - Drowned.
KIA - Killed in action.

MO - Mustered out at end of enlistment.
Res - Resigned commission.
Unk - Unknown.

Ranks are abbreviated as follows:

Pvt - Private
Cpl - Corporal
Sgt - Sergeant
1Sgt - First Sergeant
2Lt - Second Lieutenant
1Lt - First Lieutenant

Capt - Captain
Maj - Major
LCol - Lieutenant Colonel
Chap - Chaplain
Surg - Surgeon
ASur - Assistant Surgeon

MEMBERS OF THE 161ST NEW YORK VOLUNTEER INFANTRY REGIMENT

(Not a complete roster)

Name: Avery, Benjamin F.

Enlisted or Enrolled			Mustered in			Left Regiment			
AGE	PLACE	DATE	RANK	CO.	DATE	REASON	RANK	DATE	PLACE
18	Owego	1864-02-08	Pvt	D	1864-02-08	MO	Sgt	1865-11-12	Tallahassee, Fla.

Notes: Promoted to Cpl on 1865-07-01 and to Sgt on 1865-09-20.

Name: Avery, Edwin C.

Enlisted or Enrolled			Mustered in			Left Regiment			
AGE	PLACE	DATE	RANK	CO.	DATE	REASON	RANK	DATE	PLACE
24	Cohocton	1862-08-21	Sgt	I	1862-09-20	Died	Sgt	1862-11-30	New York City

Name: Avery, Gilbert F.

Enlisted or Enrolled			Mustered in			Left Regiment	
AGE	PLACE	DATE	RANK	CO.	DATE		RANK
34	Cohocton	1862-08-30	Cpl	I	1862-09-20		Cpl

Notes: On detached service at Tallahassee, Fla., when company mustered out.

Name: Avery, John A.

Enlisted or Enrolled			Mustered in			Left Regiment			
AGE	PLACE	DATE	RANK	CO.	DATE	REASON	RANK	DATE	PLACE
19	Cohocton	1862-08-30	Pvt	I	1862-09-20	Died	Pvt	1863-06-01	New Orleans, La.

Name: Ayres, Delos

Enlisted or Enrolled			Mustered in			Left Regiment			
AGE	PLACE	DATE	RANK	CO.	DATE	REASON	RANK	DATE	PLACE
19	Drydon	1864-02-23	Pvt	D	1864-02-23	Died	Pvt	1864-06-03	Morganza, La.

Name: Barbour, Charles E.

Enlisted or Enrolled			Mustered in			Left Regiment			
AGE	PLACE	DATE	RANK	CO.	DATE	REASON	RANK	DATE	PLACE
25	Horseheads	1864-02-19	Pvt	E	1864-02-19	Died	Sgt	1864-07-07	Vicksburg, Miss.

Notes: Promoted to Sgt in 1864 June.

Name: Brookins, Frederick

Enlisted or Enrolled			Mustered in			Left Regiment			
AGE	PLACE	DATE	RANK	CO.	DATE	REASON	RANK	DATE	PLACE
24	Sherburne	1862-09-25	Cpl	K	1862-10-27	KIA	Cpl	1864-04-08	Sabine Cross Roads

Name: Brown, Horace N.

Enlisted or Enrolled			Mustered in			Left Regiment			
AGE	PLACE	DATE	RANK	CO.	DATE	REASON	RANK	DATE	PLACE
21	Norwich	1862-08-29	Pvt	K	1862-10-27	MO	Cpl	1865-09-20	Fort Jefferson, Fla.

Notes: Captured at Sabine Cross Roads, La., on 1864-04-08; exchanged on 1864-10-23. Promoted to Cpl on 1864-12-01.

Name: Brown, John M.

Enlisted or Enrolled			Mustered in			Left Regiment			
AGE	PLACE	DATE	RANK	CO.	DATE	REASON	RANK	DATE	PLACE
18	Preston	1862-08-23	Pvt	K	1862-10-27	MO	Pvt	1865-09-20	Fort Jefferson, Fla.

Name: Budd, Joseph W.

Enlisted or Enrolled			Mustered in			Left Regiment			
AGE	PLACE	DATE	RANK	CO.	DATE	REASON	RANK	DATE	PLACE
20	Elmira	1863-12-15	Pvt	I	1863-12-15	MO	Pvt	1865-10-12	Washington, D.C.

Notes: Wounded at Sabine Cross Roads, La., 1864-04-08. Transferred to Co. K, 24th Regiment, Veteran Reserve Corps, on 1864-06-17.

Name: Bush, John W.

Enlisted or Enrolled			Mustered in			Left Regiment			
AGE	PLACE	DATE	RANK	CO.	DATE	REASON	RANK	DATE	PLACE
21	Cohocton	1862-08-28	Pvt	I	1862-09-20	MO	Pvt	1865-09-20	Fort Jefferson, Fla.

Name: Chaffee, Ezra

Enlisted or Enrolled			Mustered in			Left Regiment			
AGE	PLACE	DATE	RANK	CO.	DATE	REASON	RANK	DATE	PLACE
41	Hector	1863-12-29	Pvt	I	1863-12-29	Died	Pvt	1864-07-08	Vicksburg, Miss.

Name: Chamberlain, Elihu

Enlisted or Enrolled			Mustered in			Left Regiment			
AGE	PLACE	DATE	RANK	CO.	DATE	REASON	RANK	DATE	PLACE
18	Cincinnatus	1864-01-14	Pvt	I	1864-01-14	Died	Pvt	1864-06-05	New Orleans, La.

Name: Coleman, George C.

Enlisted or Enrolled			Mustered in			Left Regiment			
AGE	PLACE	DATE	RANK	CO.	DATE	REASON	RANK	DATE	PLACE
18	Benton	1862-08-15	Pvt	B	1862-09-09	Died	Pvt	1864-04-21	New Orleans, La.

Notes: Wounded in action at Sabine Cross Roads, La., 1864-04-08. Died of his wounds.

Name: Conrad, Hendrick

Enlisted or Enrolled			Mustered in			Left Regiment			
AGE	PLACE	DATE	RANK	CO.	DATE	REASON	RANK	DATE	PLACE
18	Farmersville	1864-01-02	Pvt	D	1864-01-02	Died	Pvt	1864-09-06	Transport Kate Dale

Name: Conrad, Henry A.

Enlisted or Enrolled			Mustered in			Left Regiment			
AGE	PLACE	DATE	RANK	CO.	DATE	REASON	RANK	DATE	PLACE
41	Farmersville	1864-01-02	Pvt	D	1864-01-02	MO	Pvt	1865-06-20	Alexandria, Va.

Notes: Mustered out from hospital.

Name: Couch, Charles

Enlisted or Enrolled			Mustered in			Left Regiment			
AGE	PLACE	DATE	RANK	CO.	DATE	REASON	RANK	DATE	PLACE
21	Wheeler	1863-12-29	Pvt	C	1863-12-29	Died	Pvt	1864-08-24	New Orleans, La.

Name: Craig, Willis E.

Enlisted or Enrolled			Mustered in			Left Regiment			
AGE	PLACE	DATE	RANK	CO.	DATE	REASON	RANK	DATE	PLACE
25	Elmira	1862-09-18	Capt	H	1862-09-18	MO	Maj	1865-09-20	Fort Jefferson, Fla.

Notes: Promoted to Major on 1863-09-16. Commanded regiment in Mobile Campaign.

Name: Darling, Louis

Enlisted or Enrolled			Mustered in			Left Regiment		
AGE	PLACE	DATE	RANK	DATE		REASON	RANK	DATE
58	Elmira	1862-09-15	Surg	1862-09-15		Dis	Surg	1864-04-13

Name: Davidson, Joseph B.

Enlisted or Enrolled			Mustered in			Left Regiment			
AGE	PLACE	DATE	RANK	CO.	DATE	REASON	RANK	DATE	PLACE
38	Elmira	1862-08-21	Pvt	C	1862-09-17	MO	Sgt	1865-09-20	Fort Jefferson, Fla.

Notes: Promoted to Cpl on 1863-03-06, and to Sgt on 1864-05-02.

Name: Davis, Parvis

Enlisted or Enrolled			Mustered in			Left Regiment		
AGE	PLACE	DATE	RANK	CO.	DATE	REASON	RANK	DATE
36	Elmira	1863-12-28	2Lt	F	1863-12-28	Res	1Lt	1864-06-08

Notes: Promoted to 1Lt on 1864-01-23.

Name: Decker, James B.

Enlisted or Enrolled			Mustered in			Left Regiment			
AGE	PLACE	DATE	RANK	CO.	DATE	REASON	RANK	DATE	PLACE
24	Cincinnatus	1864-01-14	Pvt	C	1864-01-14	MO	Cpl	1865-11-12	Tallahassee, Fla.

Notes: Promoted to Cpl on 1865-09-20.

Name: Decker, James B.

Enlisted or Enrolled			Mustered in			Left Regiment
AGE	PLACE	DATE	RANK	CO.	DATE	RANK
18	Owego	1864-02-09	Pvt	D	1864-02-09	Pvt

Notes: In Barracks Hospital, New Orleans, La., when company mustered out.

Name: Evans, Carr

Enlisted or Enrolled			Mustered in			Left Regiment			
AGE	PLACE	DATE	RANK	CO.	DATE	REASON	RANK	DATE	PLACE
18	Norwich	1862-08-30	Pvt	K	1862-10-27	KIA	Pvt	1864-04-08	Sabine Cross Roads

Name: Fitch, Lewis E.

Enlisted or Enrolled			Mustered in			Left Regiment			
AGE	PLACE	DATE	RANK	CO.	DATE	REASON	RANK	DATE	PLACE
20	Elmira	1862-08-21	Sgt	C	1862-09-17	KIA	Pvt	1864-04-08	Sabine Cross Roads

Notes: Wounded in action at Cox's Plantation, La., on 1863-07-13. Promoted to 1Sgt on 1863-12-17, and to 1Lt on 1864-03-01.

Name: Grant, George

Enlisted or Enrolled			Mustered in			Left Regiment
AGE	PLACE	DATE	RANK	CO.	DATE	RANK
18	Guilford	1862-09-22	Pvt	K	1862-10-27	Pvt

Notes: Wounded and captured at Sabine Cross Roads, La., 1864-04-08. Paroled on 1864-06-30. In hospital at New Orleans, La., when company mustered out.

Name: Johnson, George W.

Enlisted or Enrolled			Mustered in			Left Regiment			
AGE	PLACE	DATE	RANK	CO.	DATE	REASON	RANK	DATE	PLACE
25	Elmira	1862-08-14	Pvt	C	1862-09-17	Drown	Pvt	1864-07-23	White River, Ark.

Name: Johnson, George W.

Enlisted or Enrolled			Mustered in			Left Regiment			
AGE	PLACE	DATE	RANK	CO.	DATE	REASON	RANK	DATE	PLACE
26	Catherine	1862-09-05	Pvt	E	1862-10-25	MO	Pvt	1865-09-20	Elmira, N.Y.

Name: Johnson, Samuel A.

Enlisted or Enrolled			Mustered in			Left Regiment			
AGE	PLACE	DATE	RANK	CO.	DATE	REASON	RANK	DATE	PLACE
28	Elmira	1862-08-14	Cpl	C	1862-09-17	Died	Cpl	1863-07-30	Baton Rouge, La.

Notes: Wounded in action at Donaldsonville, La., 1863-07-13. Died of his wounds.

Name: Jones, William E.

Enlisted or Enrolled			Mustered in		Left Regiment			
AGE	PLACE	DATE	RANK	DATE	REASON	RANK	DATE	PLACE
35	Baton Rouge	1863-04-23	Chap	1863-04-23	MO	Chap	1865-09-20	Fort Jefferson, Fla.

Name: Kinsey, William B.

Enlisted or Enrolled			Mustered in		Left Regiment			
AGE	PLACE	DATE	RANK	DATE	REASON	RANK	DATE	PLACE
25	Elmira	1862-09-16	1Lt	1862-09-16	MO	LCol	1865-09-20	Fort Jefferson, Fla.

Notes: Promoted to LCol on 1863-06-13. Earlier service as Sgt and 1Sgt in Co. A, 23rd NYVI.

Name: Lewis, John

Enlisted or Enrolled			Mustered in			Left Regiment			
AGE	PLACE	DATE	RANK	CO.	DATE	REASON	RANK	DATE	PLACE
36	Corning	1863-12-25	Pvt	I	1863-12-28	Died	Pvt	1864-06-15	Morganza, La.

Name: Little, John F.

Enlisted or Enrolled			Mustered in			Left Regiment			
AGE	PLACE	DATE	RANK	CO.	DATE	REASON	RANK	DATE	PLACE
24	Elmira	1862-09-19	1Lt	F	1862-10-27	Dis	Capt	1865-09-20	Elmira, N.Y.

Notes: Promoted to Capt on 1863-12-24.

Name: Lloyd, John

Enlisted or Enrolled			Mustered in			Left Regiment			
AGE	PLACE	DATE	RANK	CO.	DATE	REASON	RANK	DATE	PLACE
27	Columbus	1862-09-12	Pvt	K	1862-10-27	MO	Cpl	1865-09-20	Fort Jefferson, Fla.

Notes: Wounded in action at Sabine Cross Roads, La., 1864-04-08. Promoted to Cpl on 1864-12-01.

Name: McLean, John

Enlisted or Enrolled			Mustered in			Left Regiment			
AGE	PLACE	DATE	RANK	CO.	DATE	REASON	RANK	DATE	PLACE
25	Norwich	1862-08-23	Sgt	K	1864-09-27	MO	1Sgt	1865-09-20	Fort Jefferson, Fla.

Notes: Promoted to 1Sgt on 1863-09-01.

Name: Merwin, John

Enlisted or Enrolled			Mustered in			Left Regiment			
AGE	PLACE	DATE	RANK	CO.	DATE	REASON	RANK	DATE	PLACE
19	Elmira	1862-08-18	Pvt	C	1862-09-17	MO	Pvt	1865-11-09	Elmira, N.Y.

Name: Murray, William D.

Enlisted or Enrolled			Mustered in		Left Regiment			
AGE	PLACE	DATE	RANK	DATE	REASON	RANK	DATE	PLACE
(not known)			Surg	1864-04-29	MO	Surg	1865-09-20	Elmira, N.Y.

Notes: Earlier service as ASur in 100th NYVI.

Name: Osterhout, Cornelius

Enlisted or Enrolled			Mustered in			Left Regiment			
AGE	PLACE	DATE	RANK	CO.	DATE	REASON	RANK	DATE	PLACE
18	Urbana	1862-08-23	Pvt	A	1864-09-18	Died	Pvt	1864-11-26	Urbana, N.Y.

Notes: Also spelled Ousterhout.

Name: Pendergast, James

Enlisted or Enrolled			Mustered in			Left Regiment			
AGE	PLACE	DATE	RANK	CO.	DATE	REASON	RANK	DATE	PLACE
29	Corning	1864-01-11	Pvt	B	1864-01-11	MO	Pvt	1865-11-12	Tallahassee, Fla.

Name: Powers, Myron

Enlisted or Enrolled			Mustered in			Left Regiment			
AGE	PLACE	DATE	RANK	CO.	DATE	REASON	RANK	DATE	
26	Elmira	1862-09-20	1Lt	I	1862-10-27	Res	1Lt	1863-08-29	

Notes: Resigned to accept promotion to Major, 88th U.S. Colored Troops.

Name: Prentiss, William

Enlisted or Enrolled			Mustered in			Left Regiment			
AGE	PLACE	DATE	RANK	CO.	DATE	REASON	RANK	DATE	PLACE
20	Pulteney	1862-08-22	Pvt	A	1862-09-18	MO	Pvt	1865-09-08	Elmira, N.Y.

Notes: Promoted to Cpl on 1864-09-01. Returned to the ranks, date unknown.

Name: Randall, William H.

Enlisted or Enrolled			Mustered in			Left Regiment			
AGE	PLACE	DATE	RANK	CO.	DATE	REASON	RANK	DATE	PLACE
37	Hartwick	1864-01-23	Pvt	K	1864-01-23	Dis	Pvt	1865-06-21	Bristol, Pa.

Notes: Wounded at Starke's Landing, Ala., on 1865-04-01.

Name: Reed, Jeremiah

Enlisted or Enrolled			Mustered in			Left Regiment			
AGE	PLACE	DATE	RANK	CO.	DATE	REASON	RANK	DATE	PLACE
26	New Berlin	1862-08-22	Pvt	K	1862-10-27	Died	Cpl	1864-07-20	Vicksburg, Miss.

Notes: Promoted to Cpl on 1864-06-01.

Name: Retan, Anson

Enlisted or Enrolled			Mustered in			Left Regiment			
AGE	PLACE	DATE	RANK	CO.	DATE	REASON	RANK	DATE	PLACE
20	Pulteney	1862-08-20	Pvt	A	1862-09-18	KIA	Pvt	1863-05-29	Port Hudson, La.

Name: Retan, Nelson

Enlisted or Enrolled			Mustered in			Left Regiment			
AGE	PLACE	DATE	RANK	CO.	DATE	REASON	RANK	DATE	PLACE
27	Pulteney	1864-09-03	Pvt	A	1864-09-14	MO	Pvt	1865-08-28	Tallahassee, Fla.

Notes: Enlisted for one year.

Name: Retan, Sylvester L.

Enlisted or Enrolled			Mustered in			Left Regiment			
AGE	PLACE	DATE	RANK	CO.	DATE	REASON	RANK	DATE	PLACE
22	Pulteney	1862-08-22	Pvt	A	1862-09-18	MO	Cpl	1865-09-20	Fort Jefferson, Fla.

Notes: Promoted Cpl on 1865-06-17.

Name: Russell, Leonard M.

Enlisted or Enrolled			Mustered in			Left Regiment			
AGE	PLACE	DATE	RANK	CO.	DATE	REASON	RANK	DATE	PLACE
18	Binghamton	1864-02-15	Pvt	K	1864-02-15	Died	Pvt	1864-05-07	New Orleans, La.

Notes: Wounded in action at Sabine Cross Roads, La., 1864-04-08. Died of his wounds.

Name: Smith, Thomas T.

Enlisted or Enrolled			Mustered in			Left Regiment			
AGE	PLACE	DATE	RANK	CO.	DATE	REASON	RANK	DATE	PLACE
33	Owego	1864-02-08	Pvt	K	1864-02-08	MO	Pvt	1865-12-13	Elmira, N.Y.

Notes: Wounded in action at Sabine Cross Roads, La., 1864-04-08.

Name: Soper, Darius A.

Enlisted or Enrolled			Mustered in			Left Regiment			
AGE	PLACE	DATE	RANK	CO.	DATE	REASON	RANK	DATE	PLACE
21	Corning	1864-02-15	Pvt	E	1864-02-15	MO	Pvt	1865-11-12	Tallahassee, Fla.

Name: Soper, Royal R.

Enlisted or Enrolled			Mustered in			Left Regiment			
AGE	PLACE	DATE	RANK	CO.	DATE	REASON	RANK	DATE	PLACE
23	Elmira	1863-12-18	2Lt	I	1863-12-18	MO	1Lt	1865-11-12	Tallahassee, Fla.

Notes: Promoted to 1Lt on 1864-01-17.

Name: Stoddard, Philo K.

Enlisted or Enrolled			Mustered in			Left Regiment			
AGE	PLACE	DATE	RANK	DATE		REASON	RANK	DATE	PLACE
38	Brashear City	1863-09-03	ASur	1863-09-14		MO	ASur	1865-09-20	Fort Jefferson, Fla.

Name: Such, Christopher C.

Enlisted or Enrolled			Mustered in			Left Regiment			
AGE	PLACE	DATE	RANK	CO.	DATE	REASON	RANK	DATE	PLACE
18	Urbana	1862-08-20	Pvt	A	1862-09-18	MO	Pvt	1865-10-17	Tallahassee, Fla.

Name: Swain, Charles M.

Enlisted or Enrolled			Mustered in			Left Regiment			
AGE	PLACE	DATE	RANK	CO.	DATE	REASON	RANK	DATE	PLACE
22	Kirkwood	1864-01-14	Pvt	K	1864-01-14	Died	Pvt	1864-06-12	Morganza, La.

Notes: Appointed Musician on 1864-04-04. Changed to Pvt, date unknown.

Name: Thurston, Frank L.

Enlisted or Enrolled			Mustered in			Left Regiment			
AGE	PLACE	DATE	RANK	CO.	DATE	REASON	RANK	DATE	PLACE
29	Binghamton	1864-02-15	Pvt	D	1864-02-15	Died	Pvt	1865-06-05	Greenville, La.

Notes: Wounded in action at Spanish Fort, Ala., 1865-03-28. Died of his wounds.

Name: Tillson, George M.

Enlisted or Enrolled			Mustered in			Left Regiment			
AGE	PLACE	DATE	RANK	CO.	DATE	REASON	RANK	DATE	
21	Albany	1862-09-29	Capt	K	1862-09-29	Dis	Capt	1864-09-16	

Notes: Wounded in action at Sabine Cross Roads, La., 1864-04-08.

Name: Watkins, William

Enlisted or Enrolled			Mustered in			Left Regiment			
AGE	PLACE	DATE	RANK	CO.	DATE	REASON	RANK	DATE	PLACE
44	Kirkwood	1864-01-02	Pvt	K	1864-01-02	KIA	Pvt	1864-04-08	Sabine Cross Roads

Name: Watson, Thomas J.

Enlisted or Enrolled			Mustered in			Left Regiment			
AGE	PLACE	DATE	RANK	CO.	DATE	REASON	RANK	DATE	PLACE
21	Veteran	1864-02-08	Pvt	E	1864-02-08	Unk	Pvt	1865-05-15	Elmira, N.Y.

Name: Wheaton, John

Enlisted or Enrolled			Mustered in			Left Regiment			
AGE	PLACE	DATE	RANK	CO.	DATE	REASON	RANK	DATE	PLACE
33	Kirkwood	1864-01-14	Pvt	K	1864-01-14	MO	Pvt	1865-11-12	Tallahassee, Fla.

Notes: Trf Co A 1865-09-02

Name: Whiteney, George A.

Enlisted or Enrolled			Mustered in			Left Regiment			
AGE	PLACE	DATE	RANK	CO.	DATE	REASON	RANK	DATE	PLACE
19	Elmira	1862-08-13	Pvt	B	1862-09-09	Died	Pvt	1864-06-05	Morganza, La.

Name: Wilson, William

Enlisted or Enrolled			Mustered in			Left Regiment			
AGE	PLACE	DATE	RANK	CO.	DATE	REASON	RANK	DATE	PLACE
24	Norwich	1862-08-23	Pvt	K	1862-10-27	MO	Cpl	1865-09-20	Fort Jefferson, Fla.

Notes: Captured at Sabine Cross Roads, La., 1864-04-08, and exchanged on 1864-10-23. Promoted to Cpl on 1864-12-01.

INDEX

4th Louisiana Native Guard	55
6th Michigan Regt	59, 61
17th New York Regt	14
23rd New York Regt	14, 86
23rd Wisconsin Regt	6, 70, 84, 85
29th Illinois Regt	6, 84
29th Maine Regt	26
30th Missouri Regt	6, 84
48th U.S. Colored Regt	54
75th U.S. Colored Regt	70
76th Illinois Regt	76
82nd U.S. Colored Regt	92
90th New York Regt	15
92nd U.S. Colored Regt	70
100th New York Regt	58
109th New York Regt	15
110th New York Regt	92
150th New York Regt	61
Alabama River	62
Alabama Welcome Center	95, 97
Alcohol	50
Alexandria	20-22, 33-35, 44 (map), 45
Alexandria burned	37, 46
Alexandria, Virginia	17
Alligators	21
Antietam, Battle of	9, 15, 43
Apalachicola, Florida	92
Appomattox Courthouse	91, 98
Arkansas	19, 24, 40, 73
Arkansas River	60
Arlington National Cemetery	103-4
Army of Northern Virginia (Confederate)	67, 98
Army of Tennessee (Confederate)	81
Army of the Cumberland (Union)	81, 85
Army of the Gulf (Union)	32
Army of the Tennessee (Union)	38
Atchafalaya River	38, 44 (map), 45, 46, 70, 71
Athens Township	14, 21

Atlanta	56, 61, 65, 67. 83
Avery John A.	32
Avery, Benjamin F.	32
Avery, Edwin C.	32
Avery, Gilbert F.	32
Avoyelles Prairie	37, 44 (map)
Awkward squad	71-2
Ayres, Delos	52
Bailey, Gen Joseph	35, 38, 46, 53, 56, 59, 88
Bailey, Thanks of Congress	35
Baltic (steamboat)	78
Banks, Gen Nathaniel P.	19-21, 29, 31, 33, 34, 40
Barbour, Charles E.	57
Barracks General Hospital	89
Baton Rouge	19, 46, 47, 62, 63, 83
Bayou De Glaize	38, 44 (map)
Bayou Letsworth	70
Bayou Pierre	23 (map), 35
Bayou Rapides	20
Bayou Sara	72
Benedict, Col Lewis	29, 30
Biscuits	69, 71
Black Bayou	20
Blockade	62, 67
Boredom	67
Bounty payment	58, 78
Bradford County, Pennsylvania	14, 101
Bristoe's Mill, Virginia	15
Bristol, Pennsylvania	89
Brookins, Frederick O.	26
Broome County, New York	14
Brown, Horace N.	27
Brown, John	57
Buchanan, Adm Franklin	97
Budd, Joseph	27
Bull Run, Battle of	9, 14, 104
Burning	34, 37
Bush, John Wesley	84

Cahawba (steamship)	63
Campti	20, 23 (map)
Canby Gen Edward R.S.	39, 53, 82 (photo), 83, 85, 88
Cane River	33, 45
Cape Florida	17
Carion Crow	30
Carroll's Mill	23 (map)
Chafee, Ezra	57
Chamberlain, Gen Joshua L.	91
Chamberlain, Elihu M.	69-70
Chaplain	57
Charleston, South Carolina	13, 83
Chase, Salmon P.	19
Chattanooga	67, 83
Cheleon	37
Chemung River	102
Chenango River	14
Christian Commission	17
Christmas	81
Clara Bell (transport)	59
Cloutierville	20
Clyde (transport)	92
Coleman, George C.	22, 27, 79
Collision of steamboats	84
Columbus, Kentucky	73, 76, 77, 78
Commissary	50
Congress	35, 102
Congressional Committee on the Conduct of the War	40
Conrad, Hendrick	17, 66
Conrad, Henry A.	17, 66
Consumption (tuberculosis)	70
Corduroy road	86
Corolla Lighthouse	96
Corps d'Afrique	20, 54
Cotton	19, 84
Couch, Charles M.	59
Cox's Plantation	16
Craig, Willis E.	76, 85, 87
Crump's Corners	23 (map)
Crump's Hill	20

D'Olive's Creek	88
Daily schedule	47
Dam on Red River	35, 36 (photo), 37
Dannelly's Mills	86, 87, 98
Daphne, Alabama	98
Darling, Lewis	58
Dauphin Island	5, 85, 62, 95, 96
Davidson, Joseph B.	24, 30, 32
Davis, Jefferson	20, 92
Davis, Parvis	49
De Glaize Bayou	38. 44 (map)
Decker, James	51
Delos Ayres	50
Dept of West Mississippi	53
Devall's Bluff	60, 83
Diarrhea	9, 46, 49-51, 70, 76
Dickey, John H. (steamboat)	84
Discipline	67
Donaldsonville	79
Dry Tortugas, Florida	92
Dutchtown Cemetery	7, 102
Dwight, Gen William	24, 25, 26, 29, 32
Dysentery	49, 51
Easter	17
Election of 1864	75
Elmira	7, 13, 16, 41, 58, 102
Elmira Daily Advertiser	24, 30, 32
Elmira prison camp	103
Emory, Gen William H.	25, 28, 29, 31, 32
Estuarium	96
Evans, Carr	27
Exchange of prisoners	74
Explosion at Mobile	92
Factors Cotton Press	17
Fairhope, Alabama	98
Fairman, Charles	22
Falls of the Red River	35, 46
Farragut, Adm David	62, 94 (photo), 95
Fish River	87, 98

Fitch, Lewis E.	22, 27, 47
Flien	34
Foraging	50, 71
Forrest, Gen Nathan Bedford	39, 73, 78
Fort Barrancas, Florida	92
Fort Blakely	65, 88, 97, 98
Fort De Russy	20, 44 (map)
Fort Gaines	5, 62, 65, 66, 88, 89, 96, 98
Fort Jackson	63
Fort Jefferson, Florida	92
Fort Morgan	5, 62, 63 (photos), 65, 96-8
Fort Pillow, Tennessee	73
Fort Powell	62
Fort Sumter	13
Franklin, Gen William	32
Franklin, Louisiana	20
Fresh fish (new recruits)	21, 77
Gaines Mill, Virginia	9, 15
Gebin	70
Gettysburg	43, 51
Gleason, Bertha	8
Gleason, Curtis	101, 102
Gleason, Cynthia Jane	103
Gleason, Lemuel Curtis	66
Gleason, Rufus B.	53, 57, 61, 102
Good Friday	17, 45
Gordon, Gen George H.	59
Grand Bayou	35
Grand Ecore	20, 22, 23 (map), 31-3, 35, 45
Grand Lake	35
Granger, Gen Gordon	62, 63 (photo), 85, 94 (photo), 97
Grant's Pass	85, 95
Grant, Gen Ulysses S.	33, 46, 52, 56, 67, 68 (photo), 74. 88, 91
Grant, George	27
Guard duty	79-80
Guerrillas	84
Gulf Shores, Alabama	97
Guppey, Col Joshua J.	70

Hardtack	50
Henderson's Hill	20
Holmes, Oliver Wendell	103
Hood, Gen John B.	81, 83
Huntington, John	57
Hurricane Ivan	97
Hussar (transport)	92
Inflation	58
Island Number 73	60
Jackson, Mississippi	56
Johnson, George W.	59-60
Johnson, Samuel A.	54, 60, 79
Johnston, Gen Joseph E.	91
Jones, Chaplain William E.	33, 57, 60, 64, 66, 83, 87
Kate Dale (steamboat)	17, 66
Kennerville, Louisiana	5, 84
Kent, Col Loren	84
Key West	17
Kinsey, LtCol William	30, 31, 53, 85, 86
Lake Borgne	85
Lake Ponchartrain	85, 95
Lakeport	85
Lee, Gen Robert E.	56, 67, 90 (photo), 91, 98
Legree, Simon	45
Letsworth Bayou	70
Lewis, John	51-2
Lincoln, Abraham	12 (photo), 13, 19, 40, 55, 75 (photo), 91, 99
Lindsley, Truman	101
Liquor	60
Little Eva Plantation	45
Little Lagoon	86, 97
Little Rock	19, 20, 83
Little, John F	25, 64
Lloyd, John	27, 57
Looting	34
Louisiana government	19

Mail	49, 69, 79
Malaria	51
Manassas, Virginia	14, 104
Mansfield	23 (map), 24, 27, 31, 32, 42
Mansfield State Commemorative Area	41-2
Mansura	37, 44 (map), 46
Marksville	20, 37, 38, 44 (map), 46
Maury, Gen Dabney H.	88
McClellan, Gen George B.	75 (photo)
McDaniel, John	15
McLean, John	57
McMillan, Co James W.	29
McPherson, James	51
Memphis	39, 60, 73, 77, 78, 79, 83
Merwin, John	21, 26, 33, 45, 83, 91
Military Division of West Mississippi	39, 78
Minié bullet	9, 15, 98
Mississippi River National Cemetery	57
Mississippi Sound	85, 95
Mobile	83, 85, 88
Mobile Bay	5, 61, 62, 64, 65, 85, 95, 96
Monett's Ferry	20, 33
Montgomery, Alabama	85
Moreauville	37, 46
Morgan, Gen John Hunt	15
Morganza Bend	31, 46, 47, 52, 53, 61, 62, 63, 66, 67, 70, 72, 74
Morganza Spillway	46
Mosquitoes	22, 64, 65
Murray, William D.	58
N.P. Banks (transport)	92
Nashville	83
Natchez, Mississippi	53, 61, 73, 83
Natchitoches	20-22, 23 (map), 31, 33, 43
National Cemeteries	52
National Guard	13
Navy Cove	86, 97
New Orleans	16, 17, 21, 39, 41, 47, 62, 63, 70, 83, 84, 85, 89, 95
New Recruits	21, 77
New York State	13, 41, 78
New York Times	39

New York Tribune	28-30, 43
Nims' battery	25, 30
Northern Light (transport)	89
Northwest Louisiana State University	45
Official Record	28, 72, 83, 86, 103
Ohio State Penitentiary	15
Orcutt Creek	102
Osterhout, Cornelius	64, 70
Otis Hall (steamboat)	85
Outer Banks of North Carolina	96
Oyster Bay	97
Oysters	65
Paducah, Kentucky	73
Palm Sunday	17
Parole	74, 92
Parrott gun	30
Pay	58, 78
Paymaster	77
Peabody (transport)	92
Peach Orchard	42
Pearsall, Uri B.	35
Pecan trees	45
Pendergast, James	69
Pensacola Bay	92
Pension	2, 74, 83, 101-103
Petersburg, Virginia	67
Peterson, Sally Josephine	101
Pierre Bayou	23 (map)
Pine woods	22, 87
Plantations	21, 45
Planter (steamboat)	5, 85, 95
Pleasant Grove	7, 23 (map), 25, 27, 28, 32, 42, 51
Pleasant Hill	23 (map), 24, 27-29, 32, 43
Pneumonia	51
Poinbeauf, Dr Eugene C.	43, 99
Poinbeauf, Margie	43
Point Misery	64
Port Crane Cemetery	8, 14
Port Hudson	16, 46, 62, 63, 97

Port Hudson National Cemetery	46, 52
Portage Creek	97
Porter, Adm David D.	19, 32-35, 36 (photo), 37, 40, 45
Postage stamps	69
Powers, Myron	55
Prayer Meeting	32, 49, 57, 85
Prentiss, William	88-9
Prisoners	26, 27, 31, 38, 61, 74, 79
Raine, John (steamboat)	84
Raleigh, North Carolina	91
Randall, Albert	6, 8, 101
Randall, Andrew	15
Randall, Anna	101
Randall, Bertha Jane	6, 8, 101, 102
Randall, Clarinda Eunice	101, 102
Randall, Curtis	101, 103
Randall, Cynthia	6, 10, 13-15, 55, 57, 58, 78, 101-3
Randall, Ellis	9, 14, 86
Randall, Freeman	14
Randall, Frederick	9, 14, 15
Randall, George Henry	2, 101
Randall, Ida	8, 14, 101
Randall, John	15
Randall, Levi	15
Randall, Lyman	15
Randall, Nehemiah	2, 7, 8, 14
Randall, Olive	14
Randall, Sally	101
Randall, Truman	8, 14, 101, 103
Randall, Wesley	9, 14, 104
Randall, West	15
Randall, William A.	102
Rations	50
Reconstructed state government	19, 40
Red River	19 ff.
Reed, Jeremiah	58
Retan, Sylvester	56, 66, 78, 88
Richardson, Martha	54
Richmond	83
Ridgebury Township, Pennsylvania	101

Roll of Honor	52
Russell, Leonard M.	27
Sabine Cross Roads	7, 23 (map), 24, 27, 33, 42, 51, 74, 84
Sand Island Lighthouse	96
Sara Bayou	72
Savannah	66, 83
Schedule	47
Schilling, Judy	97
Schilling, Nicole	43
Schilling, Stephen	41, 95, 99
Segregation	55
Selma, Alabama	85
Seward Point	64
Sharpsburg, Maryland	15
Shaw, Electa Randall	56, 61
Shenandoah Valley	38, 56
Sherman, Gen William T.	20, 33, 34, 38, 39, 65, 67, 73, 91, 102
Shiloh, Battle of	43
Shreveport	20, 22, 43, 53, 56
Sickles, Gen Daniel E	51
Simmesport (Simsport)	44 (map), 46, 70
Slack, Gen James R.	87
Smith, Don	42
Smith, Gen Andrew J.	29, 30, 34, 37, 44
Smith, Gen E. Kirby	33
Smith, Thomas T.	27
Soper, Darius	49
Soper, Royal R.	21
Spanish Fort	65, 83, 87, 88, 89, 97, 98
Spruce beer	60
St. Francisville	46
St. Charles, Arkansas	60
St. James Hospital	63
St. James Infirmary	63
Stanton, Edwin M.	91
Starke's Landing	88, 89, 98
Steele, Gen Frederick	19, 20, 33, 59, 88
Steuben Farmers Advocate	25, 55, 64
Stoddard, Philo K.	58
Stowe, Harriet Beecher	45

Strip mine	43
Stuart, Gen J.E.B.	15
Such, Christopher C.	87
Sugar mills	21
Summer complaint (diarrhea)	76
Surgeons	58
Susquehanna River	8, 13, 21, 96, 104
Sutler	50, 51
Swain, Charles M.	51-2
Tallahassee, Florida	93
Tampico (transport)	92
Taylor, Gen Richard	20, 24, 32, 33, 34, 92
Taylor, Zachary	20
Tennessee (Confederate ironclad)	62
Tensaw River	98
Texas	24, 24, 42
Thetgee, Bertha	101
Thetgee, Charlotte Peterson	101
Thetgee, Robert	101
Thomas (transport)	66
Thomas A. Scott (transport)	93
Thomas, Gen George H.	81
Thompson, Cornelius	54
Thurston, Frank L.	87
Tillson, George M	27
Tombigbee River	62
Torpedoes	62
Trans-Mississippi Dept.	33
Truman, Harry S.	55
Tuberculosis (consumption)	70
Typhoid	51, 66
U.S. Army Corps of Engineers Waterways Visitor Center	45
U.S. Army Quartermaster Dept.	52
U.S. Naval Academy	97
U.S. Treasury Dept.	19
USS Chickasaw	96
USS Essex (gunboat)	36 (photo)
Uncle Tom's Cabin	45
Underhill, A. L.	64

Union Point	72
Union, New York	14
Universe (transport)	59
University General Hospital	70
Van Armburgh, Truman	14
Varuna (steamship)	16
Veatch, Gen James C.	85
Vegetables	22
Venango (steamboat)	
Vicksburg	20, 39, 46, 51, 52 (photo), 53, 56, 61, 73, 83
Vicksburg & Shreveport Railroad	56
Vicksburg National Cemetery	57
Voting by soldiers	75
Watkins, William	27
Watson, Thomas J.	49
Wellsburg, New York	7
Wheaton, John	57
White Hall Military Hospital	89
White River, Arkansas	59, 61, 76, 83, 84
White River Landing	59, 60, 73, 76, 78, 79, 80
Whiteney, George	50, 52
Wilawana, Pennsylvania	102
Wilson's Farm	23 (map)
Wilson's Landing	37
Wilson's Plantation	24
Wilson, William	27
Woodland Cemetery, Elmira	103
XIII Corps	5, 20, 24, 62, 84, 85, 97
XIX Corps	20, 24, 28, 31, 38, 51, 56
XVI Corps	20, 30, 33, 34
XVII Corps	20
Yellow Bayou	37
Yellow fever	51
Zulavsky, Col Ladislas	92